WA

CARS
THAT CHANGED
THE WORLD

50

the
**DESIGN
MUSEUM**

**CARS
THAT CHANGED
THE WORLD**

**ANDREW
NAHUM**

50

FIFTY
CARS

6   Introduction

8   Ford Model T 1908
10   GN Cyclecar 1910
12   Austin Seven c.1922–28
14   Bugatti Type 35B 1924
16   Salmson San Sebastian 1925
18   Tracta 1927
20   Dymaxion 1933
22   Citroën Traction Avant 1934
24   Bugatti Type 57 Atlantic 1936
26   Tatra T87 1936
28   BMW 328 1937
30   Alfa Romeo 8c 2900B Le Mans special 1938
32   Cisitalia Berlinetta 1946
34   Original Volkswagen 1946
36   Ferrari 125S 1947
38   Land Rover 1948
40   Piaggio Ape 1948
42   Citroën 2CV 1949
44   Buick LeSabre concept car 1951
46   Bertone BAT 1953
48   Alfa Romeo Giulietta Sprint 1954
50   Fiat Turbina 1954
52   Panhard Dyna 1954
54   Citroën DS 1955
56   Fiat 600 1955
58   Austin FX4 taxi 1956

60	Lotus Elite 1957
62	Trabant 1957
64	Mini 1959
66	Saab 96 1960
68	Citroën Ami 1961
70	Jaguar E-Type 1961
72	Lamborghini 350 GTV 1963
74	Ford GT40 1964
76	Chevrolet Corvair 1965
78	Lamborghini Miura 1965
80	NSU Ro 80 1967
82	Bertone Carabo show car 1968
84	Range Rover 1970
86	Alfasud 1971
88	Austin Allegro 1973
90	VW Golf 1974
92	BMW 3 Series 1975
94	Lancia Megagamma 1978
96	Mazda RX7 1978
98	Audi 100 1983
100	Toyota Prius 1997
102	Fiat Multipla 1998
104	Nissan Cube 1998
106	Smart 1998
108	Index
112	Credits

FIFTY CARS

The car, as we know it, may well be facing oblivion in a world trying to convince itself that it is committed to reducing carbon-dioxide emissions, and rescuing its cities from the endless sprawl that comes from suburbs at densities that can survive only with car commuting. Yet for a century, the car has been a remarkably powerful catalyst for change, whose influence can be compared easily with that of the aeroplane or microchip.

From its earliest incarnations on, the car has demanded consideration – and indeed attracted veneration – on multiple levels: as sculptural object, as the product of avant-garde industrialism, and as a remarkable piece of engineering. Thus early cars borrowed their formal expression from their nearest relatives, the horse-drawn carriages; Ford famously modelled the first car production line on the techniques of the Chicago meatpackers; and the first steps towards self-propelled mechanical motion can be found in the eighteenth century. Equally, the car has been used as a measure of national prestige – hence the successive attempts of Iran, Malaysia, Turkey, Brazil, India and China to establish themselves as global carmakers.

At the Design Museum we believe it is important to take these wider contexts into account, and not simply to focus on formal issues, no matter how seductive the stylistics can be. Our collection includes, for example, a wooden prototype of the car designed by Le Corbusier in 1928 and a Nissan S Cargo from 1987, one of the first examples of a car made by a mainstream carmaker that acknowledges the playful, emotional aspects of car design.

Deyan Sudjic, Director, Design Museum

Right: The Jaguar E-type – a British icon in car design.

FORD MODEL T

The Model T has two stories. The obvious one is that it was a sound, utilitarian device that motorized the United States. It was free from many of the quirks of other early cars, was thoughtfully engineered, and, for the time, was relatively easy to drive thanks to a semiautomatic epicyclic transmission.

Henry Ford (1863–1947) was an intuitive engineer who had trained as a machinist in Detroit and acquired a deep understanding of manufacturing techniques. But he never forgot his farmboy roots and wanted to produce a car of extreme practicality that would benefit the rural people to whom he felt closest. The flexible, well-sprung Model T was at home on the unmade rural roads that covered the United States at that time.

The Model T also has equally great significance as a symbol and advertisement for Ford's production-line techniques and became the focus of the worldwide admiration for what has since become known as Fordism. It has been suggested that the moving production line is the perfect realization of the project started in the Enlightenment to turn men into machines. Thus the eighteenth-century Scottish philosopher Adam Ferguson wrote, 'Mechanical arts succeed best under a total suppression of sentiment and reason. Manufactures prosper where the workshop may … be considered as an engine, the parts of which are men.' This could be a perfect description of Ford's integrated Highland Park factory. Intriguingly, Ford and his methods impressed both Adolf Hitler and Joseph Stalin to an equal degree.

Right above: The concrete daylight factory at Highland Park, designed by Albert Kahn, was as much an innovation as the car for whose production it was designed. The 'body drop' here, where the body meets the engine and chassis, became an iconic part of the car mass-production process. This outdoor section, photographed in 1913, must have been a temporary expedient, however. Right below: The Ford Model T – 'the car that motorized America'.

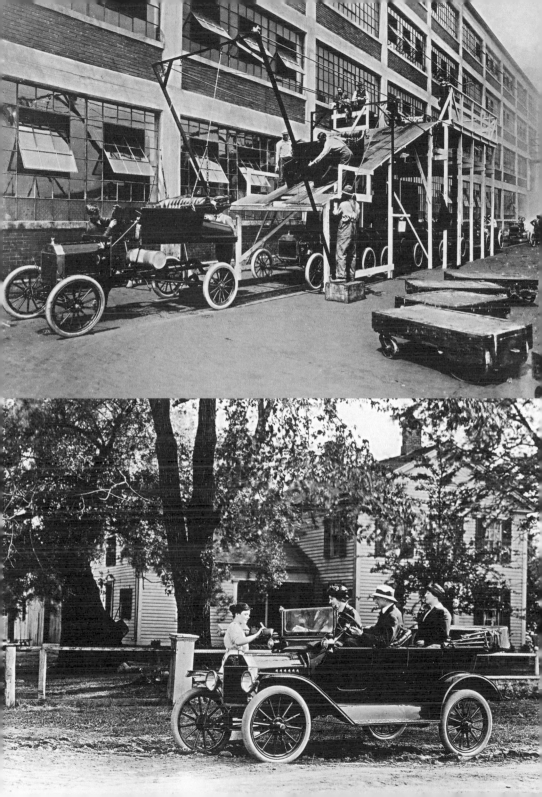

GN CYCLECAR 1910

Two car-mad young men have a dream to create their own brand. They put their design together in a parent's garage, and hey presto! – they have a popular product and an emerging motor business. So simple – and today so impossible. But not in 1911 when Archibald Frazer-Nash (1889–1965) and Ronald Godfrey (1887–1968) had just left Finsbury Technical College, London, with diplomas in engineering and set up their own company, Godfrey & Nash (GN). Their car had a two-cylinder air-cooled motor, more like a motorcycle than a car, and accordingly came to be known as a 'cyclecar'. By 1920 Archie had set up on his own, building more substantial Frazer Nash cars based on the same basic architecture.

One feature of the designs was that, instead of a gearbox, they used chains and sprockets of different sizes to give different speeds. These ran between an intermediate shaft under the driver's seat, to the back axle, and you 'changed gear' by dog clutches that shifted the drive from one chain set to another. This was quick and effective. Moreover, the car had no differential gear, because the rear axle was a single piece, and drivers of GNs considered that the cars cornered best with plenty of throttle.

The GN and Frazer Nash cars epitomized British sporting cars in the period – spindly and rakish, getting performance from lightness and simplicity. Super-sporting drivers turned them into improbably frantic hill-climb 'specials' that often beat works entries from MG and Austin, such as Basil Davenport's GN Spider, which was always suffused, in the race paddock, with the fragrant aroma of methylated spirits – the fuel it ran on. GNs and 'Nashes' also helped cultivate the generations of competitive owner-mechanics who became the backbone of that unique British institution, the Vintage Sports Car Club. An anonymous member even memorialized the inventors with this charming doggerel:

Nash and Godfrey hated cogs,
Made a car with chain and dogs.
And it worked, but would it if
They had made it with a diff?

Right above: The GN team at Brooklands for the 200-mile race in 1922. Archie Frazer-Nash is by the central car wearing a cardigan and his characteristic knitted helmet. Right below: Some home-tuned variants of the GN – such as Basil Davenport's sprint and hill-climb special Spider – were fearsomely quick. Davenport in the original Spider 1 at the speed trial on the sands at Skegness, Lincolnshire, c.1920.

AUSTIN SEVEN c.1922–28

The British-born Herbert Austin (1866–1941) had emigrated to Australia as a young man and worked in engineering, but he returned to Birmingham and founded his own company in nearby Longbridge in 1905, soon turning to the new car market. His main products were soundly engineered mid-range vehicles, but he nurtured a dream, shared by so many of the industrial pioneers in the auto industry, of making a really cheap and popular car. In spite of the fears of his co-directors, who held (as many do today) that a small car means a small profit, Austin set out to make 'a decent car for the man who, at present, can afford only a motorcycle and sidecar' and invested a lot of his personal fortune into the design.

The Austin Seven was launched in 1922 as a 'proper' small car with a water-cooled four-cylinder engine (albeit only 750cc), four-wheel brakes and a weatherproof saloon body if required. It became highly popular and soon extinguished the market for eccentric light cyclecars like the GN. Austin reflected that 'the Seven has done more than anything previously to bring about my ambition to motorise the masses'. Like Ford before him, Austin had created a new market for a new type of product.

Austin also produced many intriguing variants of the Seven, including open tourers, sports versions, full-works racing cars, and a pretty model, known as the Grasshopper, suited to the then-popular sport of off-road 'trials'.

In the post-World War II era, old Austin Sevens were so ubiquitous and cheap that building an Austin Seven special became the easiest way into racing for numerous designers and drivers. The foundations of British supremacy today in Formula One design and construction derive from the background of ingenuity fostered by tuning and adapting Austin Sevens.

Right and below: Like many car barons, Herbert Austin wanted to 'motorize the masses'. The serviceable and cheap Austin Seven proved that a properly engineered 'baby' car was feasible and profoundly altered the British motoring scene.

12

BUGATTI TYPE 35B

If Ettore Bugatti (1881–1947) had designed only one car, the Type 35B would be enough to make him immortal. His father, Carlo, was an artist, jeweller and designer of Art Nouveau furniture so Ettore studied art at the Accademia Brera in Milan. However, he was also strongly drawn to the new field of motoring and became an apprentice at the Milan firm of Prinetti & Stucchi. In 1899 Bugatti won the tricycle class in the Grand Prix of Reggio Emilia on a Prinetti & Stucchi machine of his own design.

By 1910 Bugatti had set up as a manufacturer at Molsheim, Alsace, where he produced a fascinating series of high-performance cars that had extraordinary – even perverse or archaic – features. Bugatti always refused to be influenced by the mainstream auto industry and has been called 'the last of the artist-engineers', able to build a business around his own personality and tastes. His designs were strongly influenced by his car philosophy of *le pur sang* – the thoroughbred – a reflection of his passion for horses and dogs. Indeed, his mechanical parts can often seem organic – the exquisitely forged front axle ends for the Type 35 remind us more of a wrist than a machine part.

The eight-cylinder Type 35, introduced in 1924, has been called the most aesthetically satisfying racing car ever made. It gained a phenomenal reputation because, apart from the many Grand Prix races won by the factory, amateurs, too, could buy one and win. It represents the high point of Bugatti's production, for it came at a time when his factory's meticulous craftsmanship and hand assembly could produce a significantly superior performance. Later, as Bugatti sought to keep up with the increasingly industrialized output of his rivals, the cars became more thickset and the lightness, poise and accuracy of the Type 35B were never to be recaptured.

Right: H. Heusser in the Buckower Dreieck – a triangular circuit east of Berlin, c.1924. The Type 35 was a 'catalogue racer' that you could buy and win with. Below: Original poster from 1925.

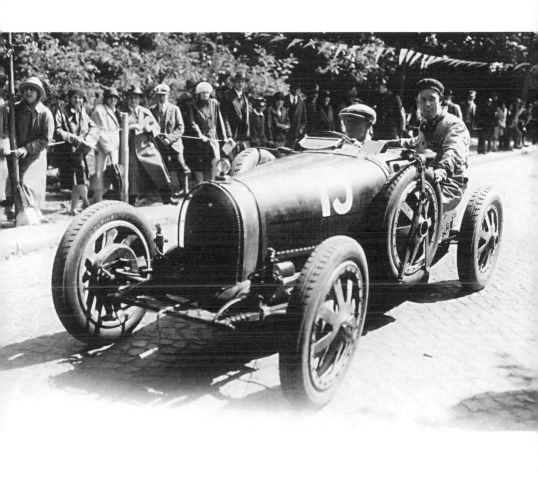

SALMSON SAN SEBASTIAN

The French were the first real *automobilistes* for they understood that this new form of mobility was both empowering and chic. During the 1920s and 1930s, there was a huge flowering of mechanical imagination as both *garagistes* and bigger factories innovated and designed new cars, though many offered eccentric mechanical features that were doomed to fail.

Levallois-Perret in the northwestern suburbs of Paris was the site of much of this engineering ferment, and there the Salmson factory inhabited a works in the wonderfully named rue Point du Jour ('Street of Dawn'), producing lissom 1100cc sports cars. Salmson was a proper engineering firm, making aero engines and industrial tools, which is perhaps why its car was the best of this new breed.

Light and elegant, with a body style that echoed the far more pricey racing Bugattis, the Salmsons were powered by a beautiful and advanced twin-cam engine and put up remarkable performances at Le Mans and Brooklands where, in 1927, the works' supercharged car could lap at more than 100mph. They were the natural competitors of the Amilcar, which had similar sporting looks but a much cruder engine. (The dancer Isadora Duncan was in fact in an Amilcar, not a Bugatti as is often said, when she died, throttled by a trailing scarf.)

Salmsons offered sports-car looks and excitement to many for the first time (MG in Britain was almost ten years behind Salmson in offering a light series-produced two-seater), and they set the scene for a type of leisure vehicle that is represented today by cars such as the Mazda MX-5.

Right: A supercharged Salmson 'San Sebastian' model. An impromptu car show at Chiswick during the Boat Race, 1927. Below: Emile Petit, the designer, with one of the works' twin-cam cars at the Miramas circuit, southern France, 1924.

TRACTA 1927

The interwar French motoring scene was peopled with colourful and inventive characters who believed they were changing the face of popular motoring. In some cases this was true. In the 1920s Jean-Albert Grégoire (1899–1992) ran a garage in Versailles that, he said, 'enabled me to live, and satisfy in a humble, but constant way, my passion for motor cars'.

Like so many enthusiasts at the time, Grégoire wanted to found his own car marque and explore his own design ideas. Grégoire's Tracta cars, made between 1927 and 1932, were among the first front-wheel drive cars offered for general sale. It is hard to realize how revolutionary a change this seemed at the time and Grégoire did much to popularize the idea, mainly through excellent performances at Le Mans and other sporting contests. Nonetheless, he remarked, 'I do not think the Société des Automobiles Tracta ever succeeded, no matter what the price was, in selling a car for more than it actually cost.'

Much of Grégoire's effort was financed by his friend Pierre Fenaille, though Grégoire later commented ungratefully that his 'considerable fortune merely strengthened his innate financial caution'. However, unlike so many small constructors, Grégoire did make a success of his business, supplying his swivelling Tracta joints for front-wheel drive to a number of civil and military users. He also had a brief and less successful involvement in the Citroën Traction Avant project.

Right above: A Tracta at the Junior Car Club trial on 8 March 1930. Front-wheel drive may have helped but the Tracta's low build also made for good performance. Right below: The waspish pointed tail was an emblematic feature of 1920s French sports cars.

DYMAXION

Buckminster Fuller (1895–1983) was a self-appointed architect, highly original thinker and compelling speaker who was committed to arguing his personally imagined 'rational' future into being, sometimes in four-hour lectures. Part of this vision included new industrial system-built houses for which he coined the name 'Dymaxion', a term that feels at once beckoning, scientific and indecipherable. Of course, the inhabitants of these new living units were to have a flying car and, accordingly, the first Dymaxion car design shows stubby inflatable wings. As built, the car was wingless but was intended to raise its tail and 'plane' on two front wheels – a tendency that made it hard to control at speed; the rear-wheel steering made it difficult to control when going slow, too!

At a time when mainstream automakers were experimenting with both rear engines and rear-wheel drives or front engines plus front-wheel drive, the Dymaxion bucked all the trends by having, uniquely, a rear engine and front rear-wheel drive. Unfortunately, the prototype was involved in a fatal accident at the 1933 Chicago World Exposition, though this may not have been connected with the unconventional aspects of the design.

The car should perhaps be regarded more as a piece of Modernist polemics than as a practical vehicle. Togther with the weird body design devised by Walter Gropius for Adler, the Dymaxion proved for ever that architects should not meddle with automotive design.

Right and below: The shape of the future? There is something at once admirable and sad about Buckminster Fuller's quixotic attempt to remake the world.

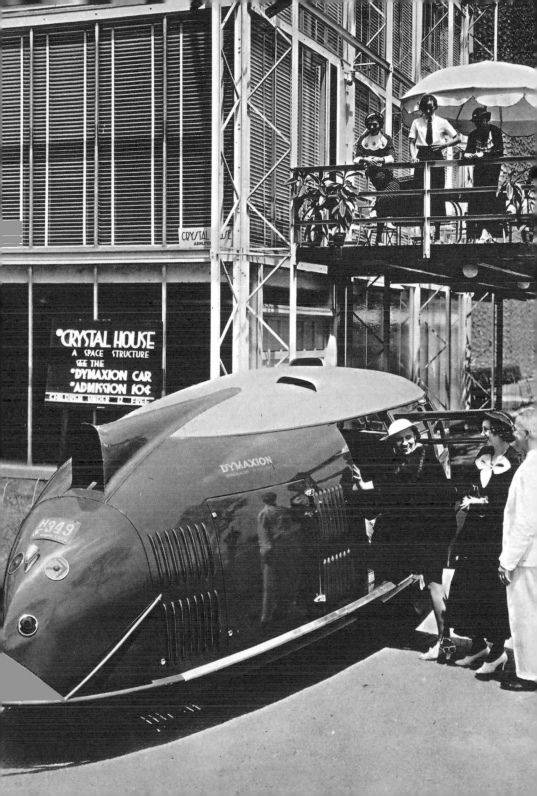

CITROËN TRACTION AVANT 1934

André Citroën's first business venture, at the age of 22, was making 'chevron' gears with special V-shaped teeth – still represented on the Citroën logo. A brilliant industrialist, engineer and financial gambler, Citroën (1878–1935) was intensely interested in industrial technique and in the methods of Henry Ford, which he saw in the United States in 1912. He was inspired by this latter experience to start and run a successful armaments factory in Paris during World War I.

After the war, Citroën returned to automobiles, arguing that the future did not lie with expensive hand-built cars (such as those of Mors, the company for which he had worked before the war) but with an affordable and reliable mass-market product. For him, the car was 'not an instrument of luxury but essentially an instrument of work'.

Accordingly, he converted the munitions plant on the Quai de Javel for car production, assembling an extraordinarily talented team, including chief engineer André Lefèbvre (1894–1963), a graduate of the Ecole Supérieure d'Aéronautique who had previously worked for the eccentric aviation and auto pioneer Gabriel Voisin. 'When you throw a hammer, it is the head, not the handle that travels first,' Lefèbvre argued in support of front engines and front-wheel drive.

The new mid-range car, the Traction Avant, had front-wheel drive, remarkable roadholding, and excellent strength and durability. Moreover, it combined advanced French engineering with the latest US production techniques, for it was the Edward G Budd Company of Philadelphia, the great pioneer of chassis-less all-steel welded car bodies, that produced the press tooling and body engineering scheme to make it. How this collaboration was arranged in the age of the transatlantic steamer is a story that still needs to be told, but it produced the basis for the modern family car.

Right: The body style of the Onze Léger, or 'Traction', respected the styling that was normal before World War II. However, its rigid pressed-steel body, weight bias to the front, and front-wheel drive made it the archetype of the modern mid-size European saloon.

BUGATTI TYPE 57 ATLANTIC　　1936

By the mid-1930s the Bugatti factory in Alsace could no longer live on sales of skinny, swift, nervous near-racers so developed a market for a more civilized high-speed sports car.

The Type 57 was generally more conventional than previous Bugattis and owed much to Ettore Bugatti's eldest son, Jean (1909–39), who was talented, active and not as stubborn as his father about adopting necessary trends from the mainstream auto industry. In fact, Jean Bugatti was in effective control of the factory from 1936, for Ettore, embittered by a strike and growing communist militancy at the factory, had largely decamped to Paris where he worked on his new and successful railcar business and his own design of racing aircraft.

Jean Bugatti would no doubt have continued the success of the Bugatti marque had he not been killed while testing a racing version of the Type 57 near the works in 1939. The fact that this occurred at ten o'clock at night on the open road to Strasbourg, supposedly closed and policed by employees from the factory, speaks of the unusual organization of the firm. Sadly, a cyclist evaded or ignored the helpers and Jean hit a tree as he veered to miss him.

The Atlantic really represents the epitaph on the original Bugatti enterprise. After Jean's death, Bugatti design entered a twilight phase. There were no really new designs and no ruling genius to revive the firm after the war. The special Atlantic body on some Type 57s was Jean's own creation and, while not as fluid as the aerodynamic coachwork being created in Paris for firms such as Delage and Delahaye, it is a wonderful and almost eccentric marriage of the streamline idiom with the classic sports racing car.

Right and below: Bugatti's coachwork for his ultra-rapid Type 57.

TATRA T87

1936

The Zeppelin airships used in World War I were responsible for Germany's early interest in streamlining – the aerodynamics of these big structures needed careful treatment if they were to reach a reasonable speed. With the end of the war and enforced disarmament, Zeppelin engineer and aerodynamicist Paul Jaray (1889–1974) set out to apply the new science of streamlining to cars, eventually setting up the Jaray Streamline Carriage Company in Zurich, Switzerland.

In 1930 Hans Ledwinka (1878–1967), chief designer for Tatra in Czechoslovakia, with design engineer Erich Übelacker, decided that properly streamlined bodywork would be the next important technical development. Ledwinka was one of the great geniuses of automotive design and had already introduced now-standard items, such as four-wheel brakes and independent suspension, before many others.

To realize the ideal Jaray shape properly, a rear engine was needed, which Ledwinka liked because it made for an unusually quiet interior and dispensed with the propeller shaft between front engine and rear wheels. This gave a low floor with greater leg space, fewer power losses and higher efficiency. The early 850cc rear-engined Tatra had a highly suggestive resemblance to the first prototypes for the KdF-Wagen, or Volkswagen, and it is alleged that Tatra's successors received a substantial legal settlement from VW after World War II for design infringement.

The Tatra streamline concept reached its height with the very fast 3-litre air-cooled eight-cylinder T87. This was capable of 100 mph and was a particular favourite with German army officers – until, that is, crashes on the new autobahn system led to the Reichswehr banning the model. As Volkswagen and Porsche designs were also to show, the 'pendulum swing' of a rear engine can bring dangerous handling on fast corners. Although not fully resolved, and despite a slightly homemade feel to the body panels, the Tatra streamlined shape is a poignant relic of a vanished Middle European modernity.

Right and below: A relic of a vanished European modernity? Sadly, Tatra never recovered the prestige it enjoyed before World War II, though it did, under communist direction, go on to build serviceable trucks.

BMW 328

In the 1930s sporting British drivers were keen on the gruelling Continental Alpine Trials, which included some 1,500 miles of high-speed touring, speed runs on the new autoroutes and long full-throttle climbs at speed up Alpine passes. These events were a challenging test for cars at the time and were seen as a useful way to develop performance and durability.

Frazer Nash factory drivers and private owners from Britain did well in these events, so the arrival of a new generation of BMW sports car that often passed the chain-drive British entries came as a shock – so much so that the British firm rapidly acquired a licence to import and sell the German cars.

During World War I the Bayerische Motoren Werke had started making aero engines (the blue-and-white BMW logo is said to represent a spinning propeller disc) but postwar had gone into car and motorcycle production. The 328 was perhaps the first modern sports car with a rigid box-section chassis, new standards of roadholding and a powerful and original six-cylinder engine.

After World War II, all this fine technology passed to the Bristol aircraft company in the UK, as an element of war reparation. With this 'flying start', Bristol made some impressive and expensive aerodynamic saloons on the BMW design base, but while BMW itself recovered from wartime devastation to become the extraordinary firm we know today, the high-tech and profitable Bristol company, though cosseted by government defence contracts, became submerged in the amalgamations of the UK aircraft sector and its car production withered away – just one more mystery in the history of technological successions.

Right: The first modern sports car? The BMW 328 instantly made British equivalents seem dated. Postwar, it formed the basis for Bristol cars. Below: The original six-cylinder engine.

TOURING-BODIED ALFA ROMEO 8C 2900B LE MANS SPECIAL

There is an evocative 1930s picture of two girls at the Touring coachworks factory in Milan effortlessly holding the complete inner-body framework for a Lancia Aprilia. This is Touring's famous Superleggera ('superlight') construction system, in which a complete inner basketwork of tubes defines and supports an outer skin in sheet aluminium alloy.

Carrozzeria Touring was one of the glories of the great age of the automobile in Italy and formed a wonderful symbiosis with Alfa Romeo, also in Milan. Felice Bianchi Anderloni (1883–1948), the man who steered it, was a deep thinker, interested in both aerodynamics and structural engineering, but also chic, immaculately turned out and gifted with unerring good taste. During his early career he worked at Isotta Fraschini, rubbing shoulders with car stars such as the Maserati brothers.

The body conceived for the Alfa Romeo's 1939 Le Mans race entry represents the ultimate evolution of Touring's aerodynamic and aesthetic thinking before World War II called a halt to development. It preserves, in an extraordinary way, the ghostly outlines of the 'classical' vintage car, which seem to be morphing before our eyes into a true wind-sculpted, modern shape. After 1945, this was to be the point of departure for the Cisitalia and the postwar 'Italian line'.

During the 1950s Touring remained influential and formed strong associations in the UK with Bristol, Jensen and, above all, Aston Martin, which built its cars on the Superleggera system for many years. In terms of pure 'class', Touring was unequalled, but, sadly, it failed to transform itself from bespoke coachbuilder into a global consultancy such as Bertone and Pininfarina and the firm folded in 1964.

Right: As far as it got before World War II – performance streamlining applied to Alfa Romeo's Le Mans contender. BMW liked it so much that it commissioned a near-identical body for the 328 entered in Le Mans the following year. Below: The inner framework of steel tubes for Touring's patent 'superlight' body system.

CISITALIA BERLINETTA

When New York's Museum of Modern Art selected a Cisitalia Berlinetta for display in 1951, car designers felt just recognition had come to them at last. Architects and industrial designers were busy creating a new world, but they often denigrated the seductive tricks that car designers deployed with chrome, fins and annual model changes. The beautifully balanced Cisitalia proved that the control of automotive form was a real sculptural art.

However, there were deeper reasons, both cultural and aesthetic, that lay behind the huge reputation of the Cisitalia. For a start, Fiat's factories lay almost silent in 1945, as the front line of war swept over northern Italy, and the Cisitalia, conceived in Turin by businessman and racing driver Piero Dusio (1899–1975), represented an automotive renaissance.

On an aesthetic level, too, the car represents the resolution of the trend towards the integration of the various separate parts of old-style car bodywork that had been progressing throughout the 1930s. In the last years of peace, the Touring coachwork company in Milan had produced a marvellous streamlined body for the Alfa Romeo 8C – its 1938 Le Mans entry (see the previous entry) – but, though sublime from some angles, it was, from the side view, still quite massive and heavy in the 'shoulders'.

For the Cisitalia, Battista 'Pinin' Farina (1893–1966) took the same aesthetic roots but made them gel. The curves make a perfect appeal to our perception of aerodynamics, while the wheel arches and wings (fenders) have a powerful animalistic quality, evoking the front paws and rear haunches of a leopard at rest and speaking to some subconscious archetype of power and drive. This form was to influence the Italian 'sporting line' that Ferrari and the other great Italian marques were to use for decades to come, and even found an echo in Britain with the sporting Jaguars.

Right: The war is over and the future starts here. The perfect stance of the Cisitalia Berlinetta shows why Pininfarina still cite it as a definitive point in the company's design development.

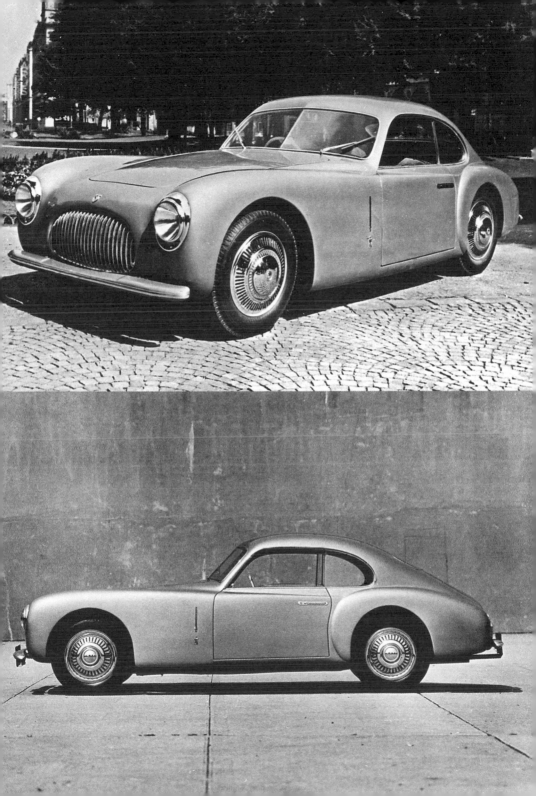

ORIGINAL VOLKSWAGEN 1946

The original Volkswagen had the longest production run of any car. Prototypes arrived in Nazi Germany in 1938, though none, in fact, was ever sold to workers saving up their 1,000 Reichsmarks through Hitler's 'Strength through Joy' scheme. Proper production began in 1946 and the final 'Beetle' was produced at VW's Mexican plant in 2003. By that time 21 million had been produced, making it, numerically, the most popular car ever.

So why don't cars look like Beetles any more? The reason is that the car was born in the imaginations of Adolf Hitler and Ferdinand Porsche (1875–1951) as a uniquely modernistic project 'to further the motorization of the German people'. As such, it had to express a strong Germanic Modernist aesthetic and the 'apparent aerodynamic' form developed by ex-Zeppelin engineer Paul Jaray and the Czech design engineers at Tatra – a make much admired by Hitler, a noted car buff. In fact, notes exist, believed to be by Hitler, from the 1933 meeting with Porsche at Berlin's Kaiserhof Hotel. Hitler has apparently sketched a generic aerodynamic Tatra/Beetle shape, though whether as a suggestion to Porsche, or as a visualization of what was under discussion, is not clear.

This Jaray/Tatra form, when squashed onto a much smaller utility car, strongly compromised passenger accommodation. Porsche chose a flat 'boxer' engine in the rear to indulge the streamline tail and also equipped the car with swing axles – a simple and bad form of independent rear suspension. These features combined could allow dangerous rear-end breakaway on greasy surfaces.

Nevertheless, the Beetle was conceived, all at once, as a single integrated engineering solution with no 'ad hoc' solutions or 'legacy' components from earlier models. The body structure was superb, rigid, watertight and corrosion-resistant, and the quality of the mechanical parts was unusually high for a popular car. Germany's preeminence in electromechanical engineering also meant that the electrical equipment (starter motor, ignition equipment and dynamo), often the Achilles' heel of most budget cars at the time, was excellent, so a Beetle always started on cold, damp mornings. The VW's success was a triumph of good engineering over questionable chassis design.

Right: There is a compelling theatre in car production lines. The VW Wolfsburg plant in 1953. The convex curves and the relief details in every panel gave the Beetle bodywork incredible rigidity. Below: The original Beetle.

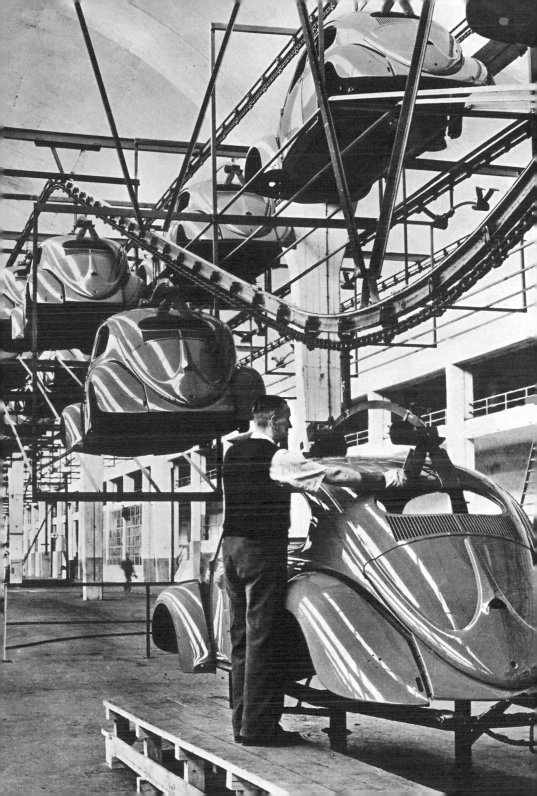

FERRARI 125S

In the morally ambiguous postwar period in Italy where accusations of fascist sympathies or collaboration flew about, Gioachino Colombo (1903–87), one of Alfa Romeo's top racing car designers, and pupil of the great Alfa Romeo designer Vittorio Jano (1891–1965), found himself suspended owing to various 'political misunderstandings'. Alfa Romeo, moreover, had had to forsake sporting cars in favour of utility products such as cookers, as well as the cheapest cars, so Colombo must have been delighted to receive a call from Enzo Ferrari (1898–1988).

Ferrari, of course, had previously run the prewar Alfa Romeo racing team. Like many engineers in the postwar era, he was forced to do utility jobs but he was itching to make his own 1500cc racing car and asked Colombo what general design principles he would adopt. 'Maserati has a first-class eight-cylinder machine, the English have the ERA six-cylinder job, and Alfa has its own 8C. In my view you should be making a twelve cylinder.' Colombo recalled the reply as, 'My dear Colombo, you read my thoughts. I've been dreaming of building a twelve-cylinder for years. Let's get to work straight away.'

The car that emerged was actually drawn up in Colombo's Milan bedroom and one cannot underestimate what an ambitious and virtuoso achievement this first Ferrari was, especially given the conditions of the time. Subsequently, some have decried Colombo's work, comparing his designs unfavourably with those of his successor, Aurelio Lampredi (1917–89), but there is no doubt that Colombo had great talent, for he later developed the Maserati 250F – the greatest Grand Prix car of its generation, and the one in which the legendary British driver Stirling Moss came to prominence. It is no exaggeration to claim that Colombo created the ancestral architecture of the entire Ferrari range.

Right and below: The first Ferrari – the 125S at the factory entrance, Maranello, 1947. We can be sure that the autocratic Enzo Ferrari was not consulted about the strident communist graffiti scrawled over the gateway.

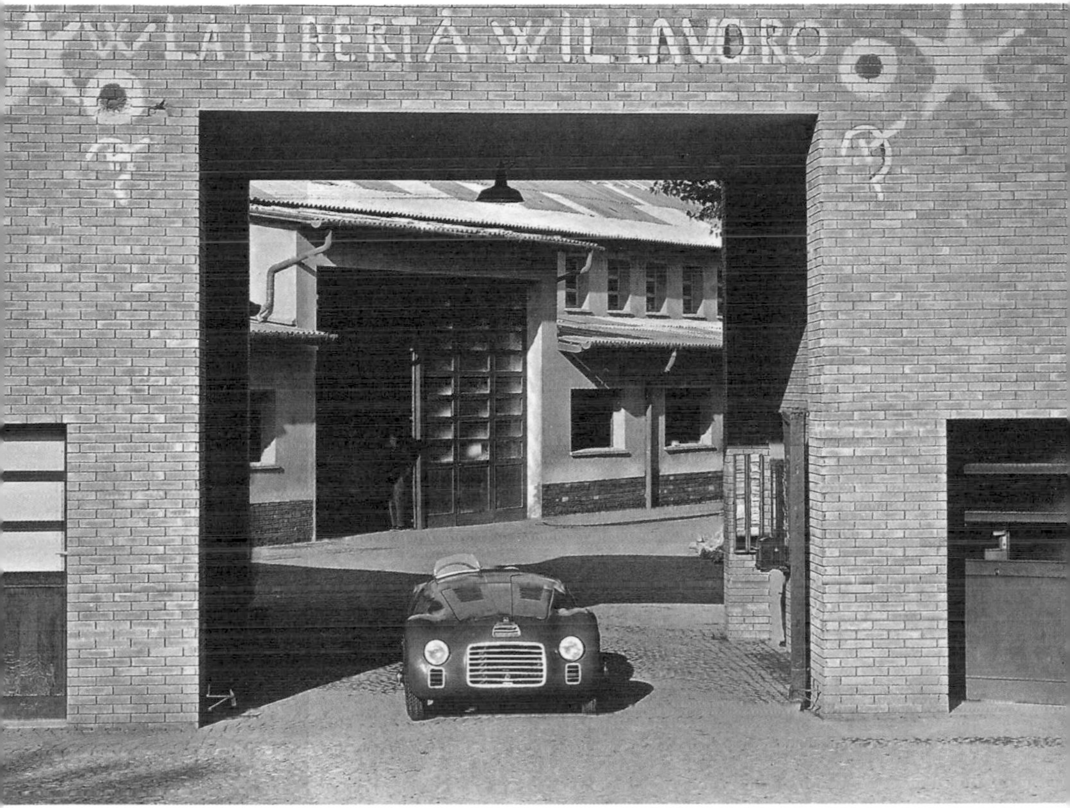
W LA LIBERTÁ W IL LAVORO

LAND ROVER 1948

The Rover company of Coventry, England, had a fine history, dating back to the 1880s when its founder, John Kemp Starley (1854–1901), invented the 'safety bicycle' – the modern, lower form of bicycle that for the first time women felt able to ride.

Rover grew as an engineering-led company, making sound, quality cars aimed to appeal to professional types, rather than speed seekers, and during World War II was enlisted to manufacture the Whittle jet engine in quantity. This tangled saga led to bitter recriminations from its inventor, Frank Whittle, who accused Rover of attempting to take over his brainchild and of making unauthorized and deleterious changes to his design. Rover handed the hot potato on to Rolls-Royce, but its amended design was an important step towards the postwar Rolls-Royce jets.

After the war, Rover returned to car production, but partner and chief designer Maurice Wilks (1904–63), who ran a war-surplus Willys Jeep on his farm, realized how useful a similar four-wheel-drive vehicle would be, especially one that was less spartan and had a greater general utility than the Jeep. Thus Land Rover was born as a British attempt to make a reliable and sturdy country vehicle. It was to use as many parts from the Rover saloon car range as possible, while body parts were mainly flat, with straight folds, to avoid expensive press tools.

The Land Rover appeared in 1948 to tremendous acclaim and by 1951 was outselling ordinary Rover cars by two to one. It had robust engineering, was functionally excellent and was decades ahead of any rival. Moreover it won extensive orders from police, military and government agencies, not only in the UK but also all around the world. The Rover company had the ball at its feet.

Right: Boxy, robust and effective, for decades the Land Rover had no rivals anywhere.

PIAGGIO APE

1948

The little Vespa-based truck that was once such a familiar sight on Italy's roads is an interesting comment on how self-indulgent much innovation can be. The tiny truck was perfectly suited to small farmers and tradesmen and was just the right size for the narrow streets of old European towns. It was also cheap to buy and, for its day, extremely fuel-efficient. Today's van driver might not appreciate having to make deliveries in an Ape. However, as large, fast and heavy as today's vans often are, they run three-quarters empty for most of their lives. An Ape with a tiny engine could often do the job.

After World War II, Italy was fertile ground for the development of new 'minimal motoring' solutions and, because Piaggio was barred from building aircraft, the aeronautical engineer and helicopter pioneer Corradino D'Ascanio (1891–1981) came up with a new, rational and integrated two-wheeler, soon to be called the Vespa ('wasp' in Italian) owing to its buzzing sound and pointed tail.

D'Ascanio's clever integrated engine and drive package, as well as the pressed-steel frame and steering arrangement, made it easy to rearrange these elements in a light tricycle truck christened the Ape ('bee'). The economy and versatility of the concept has appealed to artisans and retailers over the generations and Piaggio also has a huge production of these light trucks from factories in India, China and Vietnam.

Right: Economy and suitability for small loads. The qualities that made the Ape a favourite in Italy for small traders and countrymen also made it a hit in many Asian countries. Below: Original 1940s poster.

CITROËN 2CV

Sadly, the launch of the revolutionary Citroën Traction Avant coincided with the financial collapse of the overcommitted Citroën empire, and the final illness of André Citroën (1878–1935) himself. The control of Citroën passed to the Michelin tyre company (one of the biggest creditors), which ran the company in a singularly enlightened way for decades and drafted in, as joint manager, a former architect and World War I flyer, Pierre-Jules Boulanger (1885–1950). Tall, austere and never without a Gitane in hand, Boulanger loved driving and, like chief engineer André Lefèbvre (1894–1963), understood that the key to a fine car was good roadholding and suspension behaviour that kept the wheels in contact with the road – '*la liaison au sol*'.

Boulanger saw that France was changing and in 1936 set a brief for a 'simple spartan transport'. The rural farmer, he argued, had a right to his own special car – one with compliant suspension that could cope with the rough unmade back roads 'without breaking an egg'. What was needed was a small and cheap 'motorized pony cart … four wheels under an umbrella' that could carry two farmers wearing clogs, 60 kg of potatoes or a small cask of wine – in fact, a minimalist vehicle of a type never built before. As for the eggs, a suspension system with springs interlinked front to rear would give Boulanger's answer, the 2CV, the potential to cross rough roads smoothly at remarkable speed.

The distinctly odd prewar prototypes with single headlight and aluminium corrugated body skins were, fortunately, destroyed or hidden during World War II, but what emerged at the 1948 Paris Motor Show was far better considered. Some journalists judged it a 'grave error' but thousands of customers queued to place orders. The English car writer L J K Setright called it 'the most intelligent application of minimalism ever to succeed as a car' and this unique French icon stayed in production until 1990.

Right and below: Could anything be more French? Some see in the original O-shaped door enclosures of the first 2CVs an echo of a 'Bauhaus circle' and a heritage of ex-architect and Citroën boss Pierre-Jules Boulanger.

BUICK LESABRE CONCEPT CAR 1951

This General Motors styling exercise is emblematic of the extraordinary efflorescence of ornament and jet-plane imagery in the auto industry of the post-World War II United States. It also might be said to be a typical creation of GM's design chief, Harley Earl (1893–1969), famous for his crushingly intimidating personality and lots of pale suits, often changed twice a day. Then, of course, there is the relationship between Earl's design imagination and the development of the business model of planned obsolescence – a symbiosis that led the US car industry, by the 1960s, to what the US activist Ralph Nader has called 'a glittering pinnacle of triviality'.

However, the real importance of the LeSabre lies elsewhere. Like Earl's Buick 'Y' job of 1937, it was one of the first 'concept cars' – a new idea in the car world. Concept cars were built both to intrigue and to lead public taste by signalling what was coming soon. More importantly, these cars made real experiments with sculptural forms and motifs and enabled designers and manufacturers to see how these might gel.

At GM, Earl established technical procedures that have become fundamental to the practice of car design around the world. Most important is the use of modelling clay, a technique that frankly admits that car design is a sculptural art. GM also introduced the use of the styling bridge, a rigid measuring tool in the form of an arch that was passed over the full-sized model from front to back, allowing precise measurements of the form to be taken as 'slices' at numerous 'stations'. This data in effect constitutes a mathematical 3D model of the car and is vital for the production of the purpose-made press tools that will translate the model into series-produced steel bodies. This mathematical procedure, moreover, was an essential step in the development of the computer-modelling techniques used today.

Right: Harley Earl and the LeSabre. The sculptural complexity of the car (whatever you think of it) shows GM's incredible control of the processes of clay modelling and then transforming shapes into sheet steel – technical procedures established at GM that spread throughout the industry.

BERTONE BAT

In the 1950s the Turin Motor Show – the *Salone dell'automobile di Torino* – was an exceptional event. In a wonderful arched exhibition hall designed by Pier Luigi Nervi, the north Italian design houses vied to demonstrate their imagination and technical ability to the world's carmakers with some of the most fabulous styling exercises ever created.

Franco Scaglione (1916–93) arrived at Bertone from the aircraft industry in 1951, after a short, unsuccessful relationship with Pininfarina, and began to apply his aerodynamic ideas to experimental cars. His BAT 5 (for Berlinetta Aerodinamica Tecnica) was the sensation of the 1953 Turin show, but it was more than a sensational catch-penny glamour exercise – it had 38 per cent less drag than the 'donor' car, meaning that a 50 per cent larger engine would have been needed to give the standard Alfa Romeo the same performance. These aerodynamic ideas certainly percolated through to Alfa Romeo competition and road cars.

Scaglione was followed at Bertone first by Giorgetto Giugiaro (1938–) and then by Marcello Gandini (1938–). These three outstanding designers made Bertone, for a while, the centre of maximum imagination for the development of the postwar car, and their selection is a tribute to the judgment of proprietor Giuseppe 'Nuccio' Bertone (1914–97).

Right and below: Franco Scaglione's BAT series is a supple and fluid response to an imagined modernity that exposes the crudity of the allusions in the LeSabre (see page 44). The BAT series also speaks of the peerless skill of Torinese craftsmen in hand-forming and welding sheet aluminium.

ALFA ROMEO GIULIETTA SPRINT 1954

The beautiful Giulietta Sprint grew out of a programme by the Italian 'state industries board' to help revive the country's troubled post-World War II economy with the development of a small and popular Alfa Romeo. This was a new market for the performance-minded Milan firm and the industry board helped finance the development of the new 1300cc Giulietta saloon by selling thousands of lottery tickets. Each of the 500 lucky winners was to receive one of the new cars. Embarrassingly, when the date of the prize draw came, none of the cars had yet been completed.

The solution was to find a specialized low-volume coachbuilder to make a special sports version of the car, appease the bond winners and save Alfa Romeo (and the government agency) from scandal. Initially the project went to the Ghia company in Turin and design chief Mario Boano sketched the car. Unfortunately, Ghia could not deliver on time, while Boano was also at loggerheads with his partner, Luigi Segre. Thus the job passed to Nuccio Bertone and the final form of the Giulietta Sprint was refined in plaster, it is said, by Boano, Bertone himself, and his new stylist, Franco Scaglione (1916–93).

The car became a fantastic success, partly because it was neat and lovely, but also because, being Alfa Romeo, the engine department designed a sporting engine – a beautiful aluminium twin-cam jewel that literally sang, giving 80 horsepower at 6,000rpm – a terrific performance for 1954. It remained the basis for Alfa's smaller engines for decades to come.

The Giulietta Sprint made its debut at the 1954 Turin Motor Show and was a fantastic hit, selling 40,000 units and staying in production for 13 years. The success of this model alone virtually made the Bertone company, which developed a small-scale production line to build it. Bertone himself later remarked, 'If Alfa Romeo had known that so many Giulietta Sprints were to be built, it certainly would not have commissioned me, but would have built them in its own works at Portello.'

Right and below: A stopgap that proved a gem. The success of the Giulietta Sprint derived from the tremendous design and craft skills that were on tap in Turin.

FIAT TURBINA

In April 1954 Fiat's famous Lingotto rooftop track echoed to a
new sound – a jet wail that came from Fiat's new gas turbine
experiment. After joking that he should maybe wear a parachute,
veteran test driver Carlo Salomano took the machine gently round
the banked oval.

A few days later, the car reappeared at Turin's Caselle Airport
for some high-speed runs, and also put some laps at Monza and
Castel Furano before the Rome Grand Prix. Its potential top speed
probably exceeded 200mph, though this was never established,
and Fiat engineers, like their rivals at Rover and Chrysler, were
realizing that the gas turbine gave extremely poor fuel economy in
passenger cars. Turbina had its greatest success at the 1954 Turin
Motor Show where the futuristic lines attracted enormous interest.
Today it is in the city's motor museum.

The Turbina was a bid to investigate the new gas turbine
for road vehicles, but also to proclaim Fiat's re-emergence as a
technological force after the war years. Whereas in the UK Rover
buried its experimental turbine in a modified body shell from a
near-standard 'Aunty' model, Fiat let rip with wonderful Buck
Rogers styling conceived by visionary engineer Luigi Fabio Rapi
(1902–1977) and realized by the incomparable craft skills of Turin's
metalworkers. It was everything a wild leap of imagination should
be and proved that Futurism was not dead. Who cares that it
scarcely turned a wheel? Even today it still perfectly fulfils its
destiny to *be* a jet car.

Right and below: Handmade
in Fiat's experimental
shop, the Turbina drew
on contemporary sci-fi
iconography and promised a
future that has never arrived.

PANHARD DYNA

Aluminium production had been vastly expanded in most industrialized countries during the late 1930s for wartime aviation. The resulting post-World War II glut was a stimulus to design in many countries. One Italian designer called it the 'Mussolini metal' and the widespread availability of the material influenced products in Italy from Gaggia coffee machines to Olivetti typewriters.

In France the search for new outlets led the giant Aluminium Français concern to team up with serial automotive inventor Jean-Albert Grégoire (1898–1992) of Tracta to design an all-aluminium car for the postwar world. Eventually produced as the light and clever front-drive Dyna, the car was a new step for the ancient and august luxury Panhard make, but it was genuinely useful and had excellent economy, thanks to an aerodynamic shape and an efficient, simple two-cylinder motor.

The Dyna was an interesting design experiment at a time when no one was quite sure what a car should look like any more. Its use of aluminium, however, proved a dead end – though touted as the metal of the future, since then its use in bodies for popular cars has remained limited. Poor Grégoire, too, evidently found his path as an independent designer a struggle, commenting, 'The hard law of life … does not tolerate people receiving reward for their perseverance and labours without dealing out bitter disappointments in return.'

Right: The aluminium egg. The Dyna Panhard was an excellent and innovative entrant to the popular car market, though, like so many unusual alternatives, it was eventually extinguished by the forces of amalgamation, homogenization and globalization. In 1965 Panhard was absorbed by Citroën.

CITROËN DS

Design writers groping for gravitas are fond of quoting Roland Barthes's comment that cars are the 'exact equivalent of the great Gothic cathedrals … the supreme creation of an era, conceived with passion by unknown artists'. The French phenomenologist's later comment that the display of the DS at motor shows represents 'the very essence of petit-bourgeois advancement' is less well known, however. Nevertheless, it is more helpful, and more interesting, to comprehend the DS in its historical context – as the very essence of the French postwar technocratic spirit. This was a time when the *polytechniciens*, iron-grey hair cut *en brosse*, were rebuilding French pride with the atomic power project, jet planes and high-rise blocks.

The new Citroën project was launched with Pierre Boulanger's brief to 'study all possibilities, including the impossible'. The car was to be 'the world's best, most beautiful, most comfortable and most advanced … a masterpiece, to show the world and the US car factories in particular, that Citroën and France could develop the ultimate vehicle'. The extraordinary glazing pattern, the entirely original profile and combination of body planes, the high-level indicators coming out of the roof gutter – a feature that could have gone so wrong! – the headlamps swivelling as you steered: all pronounced that this was, indeed, an inimitable car.

Technical leader was André Lefèbvre (1894–1963) with styling input from house Citroën designer Flaminio Bertoni (1903–64). However, the greatest technical innovation in the car was the creation of hydraulic suspension by the visionary engineer Paul Magès (1908–99), who replaced the conventional springs with a self-levelling and adaptive system of hydraulic struts supplied by an engine-driven pump. Magès used the same high-pressure hydraulic system to power the steering and brakes, creating a car that felt like no other, needing only the gentlest fingertip control on the wheel to avoid slaloming onto the wrong side of the road, and a brake pedal – just a button really – so sensitive that it felt like an on/off switch. Not all drivers liked the extreme sensitivity of these controls but the Citroën response, in effect, was, 'This is the future; this is how a car should be. Get used to it!' Some drivers never could, but for many it seemed quite perfect.

Right: Citroën designer Flaminio Bertoni had an extraordinary achievement with the DS. It was all the more impressive because, unlike at Ferrari or Jaguar, there were no predecessors to allow designers and modellers to perfect its new form language. The DS sprang fully formed into the world.

FIAT 600

The Fiat 600 was conceived as a direct replacement for the front-engined prewar Topolino, which was both cramped and, by now, long in the tooth. Chief engineer Dante Giacosa (1905–96) was nudged by the Fiat management to stay with the 'orthodox' layout (front engine and rear drive) but considered that the ambition to seat four adults in a vehicle only 3.22m (126in) long – no longer than the old two-seat Topolino – could be met only either by a front engine and front-wheel drive or by a rear engine with rear-wheel drive, integrating engine, gearbox and final drive. Front drive was attractive but Giacosa was not confident about finding swivelling constant-velocity drive joints that would be cheap enough yet reliable.

Giacosa later recalled the exhilaration, as the body model took shape, of seeing 'the creamy smooth plaster … spread rapidly over the wooden framework before it hardened … I myself filed away at the initial shape to get rid of angular edges and achieve the maximum compactness.' This is interesting because it confirms that Italy was then still using classical hard gesso (plaster of Paris) for modelling, rather than the scrapeable moist-clay technique used in the United States and the rest of Europe.

The resulting vehicle was aesthetically almost perfect – an egglike, single-volume car with the utmost economy and structural efficiency of pressed-steel bodywork. Moreover, thanks to careful development it was safe to drive and lacked the fatal oversteer of cars such as the Beetle and Corvette. It was literally the car that got Italy moving again after the war and it gave rise to the architecturally similar, but even smaller, Fiat Nuova 500.

Right and below: Dante Giacosa was one of the great 'car men', with a holistic understanding of body design, powerplants and production. Fiat and Giacosa developed a mass-production aesthetic that owed little to the United States or anyone else.

AUSTIN FX4 TAXI

Travelling in a Chicago cab lurching on expiring springs and with knee room sacrificed to allow space for the bullet-resistant screen behind the driver gives reason to thank London's Public Carriage Office. This body has set design criteria for motorized taxis since 1906, though it had ruled on horse-drawn cabs since 1679. These benevolent despots have presided over a local market distortion that has brought immeasurable benefit to London cab passengers.

It's obvious that mid-sized cars are constructed to flatter and pamper the driver and that rear passenger comfort is not a priority. So when these vehicles are converted to taxis, as in almost every other city on the globe, they give a rotten experience to the paying rear-seat passengers – dank, foetid, inconvenient to hose out, awkward to climb in and out of, too low, and with poor visibility – a sickening recipe.

The definitive London cab was designed in 1956 by Austin body designer and draughtsman Eric Bailey, apparently because the in-house 'stylist', Dick Burzi, wanted nothing to do with it. Bailey referenced current Austin saloons and Anglo-American looks in the fender and body sides (he had just finished work on the Austin-made Metropolitan made for Nash in the United States), but the principal design driver was the passenger space required by the beneficent Carriage Office.

The successor to the Austin cab is the TX4, built by LTI. It has, of course, gone through various redesigns, but its genes are still essentially those of the 1956 Austin FX4 and it has remained as much a symbol of London as the double-decker bus. Long may it continue to defy globalization.

Right: The London black cab is a benign market distortion that owes its existence not to market forces but to an institution – the Public Carriage Office. Pensioner examples also grace a few other British cities.

LOTUS ELITE

Colin Chapman (1928–82) was a brilliant, charming, innovative designer, engineer and entrepreneur who arrived in frontline racing. His path to the formation of the Lotus company, and to racing car construction, was through studying engineering at University College, London, while also selling used cars beside his father's pub in Hornsey. A spell in the Royal Air Force gave him a real understanding of lightweight structures that complemented his natural left-field thinking. He deployed this whether he was designing to eliminate structure weight, blagging deliveries from suppliers on credit, or skating his way through the construction rules in Formula One.

Chapman was among the first to understand the new design rules for car performance. The car chassis and body needed to be light and rigid, preferably integrated as a structural monocoque shell, while the suspension could be softer and tuned for the correct compliance to road or track. This was pretty much the reverse of the traditional architecture used by rivals such as Ferrari and Maserati. As a result, a Lotus was often quicker despite its engine being usually less powerful.

The Elite, introduced in 1957, was Chapman's first road car made for general sale. Glass fibre had made small production runs affordable and the Elite was the first glass-fibre monocoque, with a remarkably successful body sketched by Lotus associate Peter Kirwan-Taylor. Frank Costin, aerodynamicist at de Havilland, honed the aerodynamics. Other features included racing car features such as all-independent suspension and all-round disc brakes. It also used the terrific ex-fire pump Coventry Climax engine, previously used by Chapman for track cars.

Dynamically the Elite was almost perfect, given its date. Cornering was awesome, performance was great for the engine size, and fuel economy was terrific, thanks to the low drag body. However, as a road car it demanded lots of maintenance and forgiveness. The name itself, wags and disenchanted owners used to say, told you what to expect – Lotus stood for 'Lots Of Trouble Usually Serious'.

Right: Fast, fragile, flawed … The Lotus Elite derived terrific performance from a 1200cc Coventry Climax engine thanks to its light weight and slippery shape.

TRABANT

According to the old joke, a customer walked into a Trabant dealer and asked if he could order a car with a two-tone paint job. 'Well, why not also have a Blaupunkt radio and stereo tape player, or wait a little longer', the saleman replied, 'and you can have it with air-conditioning and antilock brakes, too.' 'That's not funny,' the punter protested. 'You're making a fool of me.' 'Well,' the salesman said, 'you started it.'

But behind the image of a gruesomely utilitarian and ersatz East German car that customers had to wait years to get is a story of skill and industrial pride. Zwickau, home of the Trabant, had made the sound two-stroke DKW car since before World War II and this formed the basis for postwar developments. The two-stroke motor, though not especially efficient, was cheap to make and to maintain, owing to its low number of moving parts. A noteworthy innovation for the Trabant was the use of Duroplast – a phenolic plastic reinforced with a wool or cotton fibre filler – for unstressed bodywork components.

When the Berlin wall finally came down, thousands of East Germans and others from the former Soviet satellites used the car to stream west in search of new homes and jobs. Soon, though, their new and more environmentally conscious hosts began to complain about both the pollution of the smoky two-stroke exhaust and the remarkable persistence of Duroplast, which has defied attempts at recycling. Nonetheless, the Trabant remains the symbol of a huge structural change for Germany that few expected they would live to see.

Right: Not that pretty, but the two-stroke Trabant let Eastern European owners hold onto the precious gift of mobility. Below: Packaging for the 'Trabbie' toy, 1970.

MINI

In the 1950s the British Motor Corporation (formed by the merger of the Austin and Morris brands) was still highly profitable and adept at production. In 1956 BMC boss Leonard Lord brought designer Alec Issigonis (1906–88) back from Alvis to create a new range of popular cars.

When the bungled Suez invasion led to an oil boycott of Britain by Arab states and petrol rationing in the UK the first priority became a really small new car. Suspension designer Alex Moulton (1920–) recalled driving to meet Issigonis in a single-cylinder three-wheeler Heinkel bubble car ('simply a device for getting 60 miles to the gallon'). Issigonis sniffed and revealed that Lord had asked him to design a real economy car, but 'whatever it is, it won't have one cylinder and three wheels. It's going to have four cylinders and four wheels.'

The key to the package lay in the use of front-wheel drive, new small wheels to save space, and a transverse engine with integrated gearbox 'sharing the same bathwater'. All these were then ambitious steps for a budget car. It is often said that great designs arise from tough constraints and the target for the Mini was a compact four-seater within a length of only 10ft (3.04m). The design team recalled that it had had to fight for every quarter inch.

The Mini was designed by Issigonis with a few trusted intermediaries, who later remarked, 'We were there to do things his way.' In turn, the Mini gave rise to Issigonis's bigger and immensely successful Austin 1100. One colleague recalled that, 'None of them were committee motorcars. Just one man breaking all the rules. It's not cheap to work that way, but he revolutionized the world's motoring.'

Right and below: The expressed external seams of the Mini simplified welding and anticipated the 'Pompidou Centre aesthetic' by externalizing technical features that were formerly buried. Les wisely, Issigonis also ignored engineering convention for the underbody and early models filled up with rainwater.

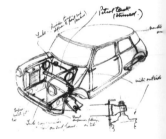

SAAB 96

The first Saab car, planned by the Saab's parent Swedish aviation company as World War II came to an end, reflects a moment of calm and privilege, far from the awful events taking place across the Baltic, and the point when the Swedish brand of Modernism finally reached auto design.

The mechanical design for the car was done by a tiny team of adept aviation engineers, unfamiliar as they were with automotive design. Perhaps for that reason, the quality of the car and its subcomponents was much higher than small carmakers elsewhere were used to providing. The Saab started out as a highly advanced but practical vehicle with independent front-wheel drive and front suspension. Unfortunately, cash constraints imposed a two-stroke engine, based on those used in German prewar economy cars such as the DKW, though the Saab version was civilized to an unusual degree by airflow specialists from the aeroengine firm Svenska Flygmotor.

The body style originated with designs from a remarkable autodidact designer, Sixten Sason (1912–67), who had a science-fiction imagination for machines that had not yet been invented. Between him and the more conservative factory draughtsmen, a rational body form emerged that is the most perfect realization of the Jaray-inspired aerodynamic European streamline Modernism. The Saab won the Monte Carlo Rally three times, proving the honesty of its design, and it showed by its durability and safety that economical cars could also offer high quality. Eventually, though, the lawnmower smell and the oddity of putting oil in the gas tank led to a switch to a Ford-built four-stroke motor.

Right above: Erik Carlsson in the Monte Carlo Rally, 1963. Right below: Front-wheel drive and independent front suspension made for an advanced package in the late 1940s when the Saab was first conceived by aeronautical engineers.

CITROËN AMI

By the late 1950s Citroën was sensing a gap in its product range between the space-age DS and the rustic 2CV. The solution was a new car based on the engine and mechanical layout of the 2CV with entirely new, more spacious bodywork that was intended, one assumes, to have had some aesthetic link with the revolutionary DS. If this was, in fact, the intention, it failed utterly, for the Ami has been called one of the ugliest cars ever made.

Its visual oddity comes from translating a formal language that belongs to a quite different type of car. The DS had a geometry that was broad, low, crablike and opulent. The Ami was pinched, high, narrow and utilitarian. However, the back-sloping rear window, which added an extra element of *grotesquerie*, was not simply borrowed from the more perverse US styling elements of the time, but was necessary to provide the cabin length required for a mid-sector car.

However, the Ami did have *something*, for by 1966 it had become France's bestselling car, though it never caught on elsewhere. Curiously, it never carried a Citroën badge, perhaps because it was plain that no other company could have made the car, or maybe because the weird jumble of converging planes and trim lines at the front left no room for one. Later, Amis were given the flat four-cylinder engine designed for the follow-on GS model, which gave them almost 90mph performance – insanely fast for this skinny eggshell.

However, in one sense the aesthetic particularities of the Citroën Ami are a delight. It is wonderful to know that there was once a time when national aesthetics were so marked and could vary so wildly from one country to another. The Ami is a poignant reminder of the days when the luxury of national identity in design was still possible.

Right and below: For all its weirdness, the Ami should be cherished, for it speaks of a time when expressing national identity in automobile design was a permissible indulgence.

JAGUAR E-TYPE

Jaguar in the 1950s was a pool of extraordinary talent. William Lyons (1901–85), at the helm, had taken the company from building motorcycle sidecars to becoming a fully fledged high-performance marque. World War II contracts for aircraft spars certainly helped improve the technical skills of the workforce, so Jaguar used argon-arc aluminium welding on its postwar light-alloy structures. During the war, too, the basic design for the magnificent six-cylinder 3.4-litre XK engine was established by principal engineer William Heynes (1904–89), supposedly while on fire-watching duty during air raids. This robust, beautiful and powerful unit was developed after the war by ex-Bentley engine maestro Walter Hassan with tuning wizard Harry Weslake and was to underpin Jaguar's racing and road car programmes for decades.

In 1948 the new Jaguar XK120 was the star of the London Motor Show, beginning a serious commitment to sports car racing that culminated in the sensuous D-Type and its numerous Le Mans victories. The D-Type body was developed by Loughborough-trained aerodynamicist Malcolm Sayer (1916–70), who brought his wartime design experience with the Bristol Aeroplane Company to bear, using closely guarded mathematical techniques. There may have been an element of 'snake oil' in his secret tables but, though rival cars were often more powerful, the Jaguars usually had the highest top speed. Sayer was also far ahead of his contemporaries in realizing that aerodynamic goals included defeating lift at high speed, and in giving his cars good stability from side wind gusts.

The E-Type is, in a sense, the road-going heir to the D-Type – a road car that looks like a racer. Although unkindly called a 'tart trap' by some at the time, it inherited the excellent aerodynamic performance of the D-Type and offered 150mph performance for half the price of a Ferrari or an Aston Martin. The E-Type was a true cut-price supercar – a 1960s British icon offering great looks and authentic engineering.

Right and below: A true cut-price supercar? The E-Type has sensuous bodywork and bulletproof engines. It made Jaguar a special brand. However did such a terrific advantage slip away?

LAMBORGHINI 350 GTV 1963

When Ferruccio Lamborghini (1916–93) complained about shortcomings in the Ferrari he had bought, Enzo Ferrari (1898–1988) is said to have remarked, 'What does a tractor manufacturer know about sports cars?' True or not, Ferrari road cars at that time, for all their speed, were doubtless carelessly made in many respects, and have even been referred to simply as 'a cynical way to finance the racing team'. Lamborghini, on the other hand, went on to show that he knew a thing or two about cars.

An industrialist and tractor-building millionaire, Lamborghini, took on the task of creating a 'supercar' with immense seriousness, building an impressive new factory and assembling a strong design and development team from the incredible network of high-performance car experts that northern Italy had on offer.

The fabulous Lamborghini V12 engine, both sculptural and effective, was the work of Giotto Bizzarrini (1926–), who had formerly worked at Ferrari, though some reports, perhaps mischievously, suggested a consultancy involvement from Honda. However, when the car was first shown at the 1963 Turin Motor Show, the engine had not yet been installed, so Lamborghini apologized for not being able to open the door or hood, exclaiming, 'My mechanic has forgotten the keys, the *cretino*!'

The styling of this first model was entrusted to former Bertone designer Franco Scaglione (1916–93) and was a little odd, the front end reflecting, perhaps, the Chevrolet Corvette Sting Ray. Even a loyal company history admits that 'approval of its styling was by no means unanimous'. But on the road the 350 was really good and, cleaned up stylistically by Touring of Milan, allowed Lamborghini to do what many have tried but few have achieved – to create an enduring new supercar brand.

Right: Too futuristic? Too American? Too odd? The new Lamborghini 350 GTV with body by Franco Scaglione, launched in October 1963, didn't cut it. But the bones of the car were good and Touring of Milan transformed it into a credible GT car that marked the birth of the brand (below).

FORD GT40

Did Henry Ford II (1917–87) decide to go sports car racing and beat Ferrari out of pique, when Enzo Ferrari (1898–1988) pulled back from a deal to sell out to the Americans in 1963? Ford certainly seemed to have regarded control of his racing teams as a plum part of the deal, for the ultimate sticking point, Ferrari recalled, was Ford's desire to control the whole race programme and leave him no discretion to spend anything over $10,000 without reference to Detroit.

Whatever the motivation, Ford decided that winning Le Mans, the world's preeminent sports car race, was a prestige worth investing in and the GT40 programme was set up by top executive Lee Iacocca explicitly to do this. Ford reached outside the company to set up a group full of talent and race experience with Eric Broadley (1928–), founder of Lola Cars and one of the great generation of British race car engineers that also produced Colin Chapman of Lotus. Veteran US racer and car builder Carroll Shelby (1923–) was also hired, along with former Aston Martin race team manager John Wyer (1909–89). The first cars were based on the Lola GT, which also used a beefy Ford eight-cylinder motor and were British-built.

Although the GT40 first raced in 1964, it did not win at Le Mans until 1966, but it then went on to win and beat Ferrari four times in a row – a feat that seemed extraordinary at the time. In 2004, under the influence of design chief J Mays (1954–), Ford produced the GT – a re-engineered homage to the GT40 as part of his 'Retrofuturism' programme. It is a fine car but not as beautiful as the original. The extra three inches of height, needed today to make it a practical road car, give a surprising impression of added bulk. Sometimes, it seems, you just can't go back.

Right above: Gold Cup Oulton Park, Cheshire, 1967. Ford could not have beaten Ferrari at Le Mans alone – it recruited racing professionals from the UK and United States to the programme to ensure success. Below: After Ford's victories, team manager John Wyer took over the GT40s and ran them with Gulf Oil sponsorship, winning Le Mans twice (1968 and 1969) with the same car.

CHEVROLET CORVAIR

When US consumer Ralph Nader published his revolutionary attack on the auto industry *Unsafe at Any Speed* in 1965, his list of unsafe cars led with the Corvair, singled out for its known record of often-fatal 'single vehicle' accidents. Compounding the corporate irresponsibility evident in the design itself, Nader argued, was General Motors's private knowledge of the car's handling problems. He claimed that, for several wasted years, the company had refused to acknowledge the problem, instead blaming driver error, and had thus delayed installing vital suspension modifications.

Ironically, the Corvair had initially been launched to great acclaim – as a mid-sized compact alternative to the large US sedans that could win back sales from imported cars. The architecture of the Corvair was influenced by GM chief engineer Edward Coles's admiration for the VW Beetle. Like the Beetle, the larger and sportier Corvair had a rear air-cooled engine and swing axles – a cheap form of independent rear suspension. Together, these brought the same treacherous handling characteristics of the Beetle, though the Corvair was a much faster and therefore also a much more dangerous car. In tight, fast bends, the wheels would tuck under the car, reducing rubber contact, and the engine-heavy rear would swing round 'like a hammer on a string', leaving the driver powerless to control it.

Between them, Nader and the Corvair launched consumerism and changed for ever the relationship between customer and manufacturer.

Right: It all started out so well. The Corvair had lots going for it – sharper styling, smaller size, but the Volkswagen-influenced rear engine brought a sting in the tail.

LAMBORGHINI MIURA

There was a moment in the history of the world when a rock drummer, or an Italian air-conditioning millionaire, could leave home scrunching the gravel on his oval drive, put in some psychedelically mind-warping high-speed kilometres, and scrunch up another oval drive in Monaco, Mentone or St Moritz. For the purpose, the world's best automotive engineers created the perfect instrument for the connoisseur driver, a mid-engined car that obediently rewarded every input and intention. Unleashing four litres of bellowing Italian performance engineering, inches behind your neck, and guzzling fuel through a dozen massive Bologna-built Weber carburettor barrels, seemed an almost blameless act in an age before issues of global warming came to light. The oval drives were important because the rear view in the Lamborghini Miura was awful and reversing a nightmare.

As part of the bid to outdo Ferrari in a true super-sports car, Lamborghini set out to use race technology and solutions to create the preeminent road-going GT car. The body followed the pattern of the Ford/Lola GT40, being an integrated structural monocoque. The mid-engine solution came from contemporary sports car racing, to give perfect balance, and the race-bred independent suspension was as smart and faithful as you could get.

All this would have counted for little if the car had been ugly but, remarkably, it had the attention of the two best design talents in the business. Giorgetto Giugiaro (1938–) had recently left Bertone, the design consultancy that was developing the body shape for the new Lamborghini, leaving a new mid-engined project on the stocks, but his successor, Marcello Gandini, finished it and turned it into the Miura. Particularly striking is the way the swelling of the rear wing (fender) echoes that of the front, like waves in the sea, and just as the Cisitalia set the form for sports cars for decades, so did the Miura for the new mid-engined layout – echoes of it were evident in the Ferrari Dino and even the more recent Lotus Elise.

Right: The Miura set a new classical standard for the mid-engined performance car in the way Cisitalia had done earlier for front-engined sports cars.

NSU RO 80

The NSU Ro 80 represents a failed revolution. The new engine concept unveiled by the unusual engineer Felix Wankel (1902–88) in 1954 was a response to an ancient ambition among inventors to create an 'ideal' smooth rotary engine without up-and-down piston movement. Wankel sold the concept to the German NSU company, which then used it to build both motorcycles and small cars.

Wankel considered himself the third in a line of great German internal combustion engineers, following Nikolaus Otto (1832–91) and Rudolf Diesel (1858–1913). Surprisingly, though, he was not interested in close collaboration with NSU – once it had bought his patents – and remained aloof as it began to turn the invention into a practical thing.

The Wankel engine was turbine-smooth and looked, to many, like the future. NSU entered into manufacturing agreements with car companies around the world, including General Motors and Citroën (GM committed a reported $50 million to its licence). NSU showcased the new motor in the Ro 80 – a new mid- to luxury-level saloon. Voted 'Car of the Year' by motoring writers, it was highly advanced in conception and performed beautifully in every way. However, the engines, which had worked well in prototype testing, failed so often in service that German Ro 80 drivers used to hold up one, two or three fingers when passing each other to show how many engines they'd had under guarantee.

Eventually, the company gave up the unequal struggle and the NSU name was allowed to fade, out of embarrassment perhaps, while the partner Audi brand was reinstated. The Wankel may have proved a disaster, but selling licences perhaps underpinned the success of Audi today.

Right and below: A marvellous car – shame about the engine. How the faults of the Wankel motor escaped detection in prototype testing is one of the enduring mysteries of automotive history.

BERTONE CARABO SHOW CAR 1968

The Italian Marcello Gandini (1938–) remains one of the most extraordinary talents in the world of car design. He followed Giorgetto Giugiaro (1938–) as chief designer at Bertone and, with the completion of the Lamborghini Miura, showed that he could work in a 'studio' style – the Miura follows closely the language that Giugiaro had established at Bertone with the Corvair Testudo and Alfa Romeo-based Canguro.

Gandini's subsequent design experiments, however, revealed a quite new aesthetic language with concept cars such as the original Stratos and the Carabo. These cars broke with the classic postwar Italian line established by the Cisitalia. They did not reference existing or historic trends but sprang into a new aesthetic world looking, it was once said, 'like they had just landed – and on the wrong planet'.

The Carabo is clearly a step towards the Lamborghini Countach that Gandini was soon to design. Even his great professional rival, Giugiaro, called him 'unbeatable at creating way-out sport cars with overpowering aggression: some of his coupés seem to bite the ground even when they are standing still'. But though aggression in cars now seems both delinquent and old-fashioned, the Carabo and the Countach should still be relished as kinetic sculptures from another age.

Right and below: The Carabo illustrates the unparalleled imagination that Marcello Gandini deployed to reinvent the supercar. He went on to extend this theme to the Lamborghini Countach.

RANGE ROVER 1970

Almost from the inception of the Land Rover, brothers Spencer (1891–1991) and Maurice (1904–63) Wilks, who ran Rover, considered making a more civilized vehicle with high standards of ride, quietness and performance on the road – qualities that the sluggish but dependable Land Rover lacked.

During the 1950s two unlovely prototype 'Road Rovers' were developed but the idea did not progress until Charles Spencer ('Spen') King (1925–) took up the project. King was a former Rolls-Royce engineer and nephew of the Wilks brothers. The challenge, he saw, was to produce a new product that could be tooled up 'for hardly anything at all … engineered from nothing'. King laid out the basic architecture of the car, while Rover exterior designer David Bache (1925–94) did a restrained and intelligent job on the exterior.

The new vehicle was also to have excellent off-road performance, and King pioneered both full-time four-wheel drive and extremely soft, long-travel suspension. Until then, Land Rovers and imitators had used hard but durable springing. This compliant suspension was a new (and better) solution for off-road vehicles and the Range Rover has consistently remained best in its class for off-road work.

Although Spen King later regretted the transmutation of off-road sport-utility vehicles (SUVs) into status symbols for city centres, his Range Rover established a new, popular vehicle segment. But its success prompts the question as to why inspired products, committed engineers like the Wilks brothers and a talented successor in King were unable to create and sustain the type of industrial auto dynasties that the Porsche and Piëch families achieved in Germany. It's hard to resist the conclusion that, by the 1970s, the milieu in Britain was just too antithetical to industry.

Right: The world at its feet. The Range Rover was the original and best on-road/off-road 4X4.

ALFASUD

Rudolf Hruska (1915–95) was one of the most engaging and talented 'car men' in the postwar Italian scene. Austrian-born, he had joined Ferdinand Porsche's bureau in 1938 as a design engineer and helped with design and production planning for the new Volkswagen. At the end of the war, he was cut off in Italy, working with Officine Meccaniche (OM) on a Porsche-designed tractor, but through racing contacts such as Tazio Nuvolari he found his way to Cisitalia and became woven into the fabric of the Italian motor industry. By 1951 he was consulting for Alfa Romeo.

After a spell with Fiat he shouldered the task of creating a new popular Alfa Romeo as well as the factory to make it – at Pomigliano d'Arco, near Naples. In part the project was intended by the government to encourage employment in southern Italy, though Alfa Romeo also considered that the company was reaching the limit of the labour force available in Milan.

For the Alfasud, Hruska used a flat-4 'boxer' engine, which he liked from his Volkswagen experience for its flat profile. To design the body he brought in Giorgetto Giugiaro (1938–) for what was to be his first mass-market success and which established Italdesign in its current premises in Moncalieri, Turin. The car itself was delightful, being marred only by poor corrosion performance in northern countries. However, the production record of the car was low, running at about 50 per cent of the target. As in the UK and elsewhere, transplanting car production to provide employment proved tricky.

Right and below: Pretty, practical and a joy to drive, the 'Sud was let down only by the enthusiasm with which the shell turned to rust. The job confirmed Giorgetto Giugiaro as a major independent designer for the industry.

AUSTIN ALLEGRO 1973

By the mid-1960s the finances of the British Motor Corporation were crumbling and the company needed serial government bailouts. To prime minister Harold Wilson and industry minister Tony Benn, a merger with the Leyland truck and bus company, led by the dynamic 'super export salesman' Donald Stokes (1914–2008), seemed the way ahead. In fact, the new Stokes empire swept up almost all the UK makers including Jaguar, Triumph, Daimler and Rover, along with the BMC conglomerate (chiefly comprising Austin and Morris brands), in an attempt to bring order and rationality to the ailing UK car industry.

The Allegro was a much-needed attempt to bring in a new mid-sized car by radically updating Issigonis's excellent, but now ageing Austin/Morris 1100, which was losing sales badly to the Ford Cortina. With Alec Issigonis sidelined, newly imported ex-Ford designer Harris Mann (1937–) drew up a decent and fresh-looking replacement, but the process of internal engineering negotiations soon pulled the concept apart.

The final result was lacklustre in appearance but dynamically not bad – though inferior to the 1100, thanks to engineering compromises on the suspension. Its novel, squared-off steering wheel, promoted as the 'Quartic' wheel, was seized on by journalists as a symbol of the futile exercise in innovation that typified the car.

Overall, the Stokes programme failed to rationalize the UK car sector with its many overlapping models, engine producers and supplier lines. The postwar dispensation in which government industry ministries had given both broad direction and major national investment to companies was fading away, while labour relations were almost uniformly awful, with the Longbridge Austin plant sometimes suffering three or four separate strikes in a day. Perhaps no one could have reshaped this crumbling archipelago, but the Allegro, in particular, has been called 'the vital stumble'.

Right: Poor old Allegro. Its general proportions were not all that different from those of the Alfasud (see pages 86–7), which everybody liked, showing just how subtle and challenging car design is.

VW GOLF

During the 1960s and 1970s Volkswagen tried desperately to find successor products to the enormously popular Beetle. The Fastback estate car (also called the Variant) was only a limited success and it amplified the potentially dangerous handling qualities of the VW rear-engine set-up in a faster car. The front-engined, but lacklustre, K70 saloon, taken over from an NSU design, also achieved only modest sales and it seemed hard to switch existing VW fans from their loyalty to the quirky Beetle or to win new customers for newer, more conventional designs.

Bringing in Giorgetto Giugiaro (1938–) was an inspired move in breaking out of this impasse. Giugiaro had just made a great success of the Alfasud, which showed he was not only a master at designing beautiful, fantastical sports cars, but also soundly practical mass-market saloons. However, also crucial to his success with the Golf, and indeed to the entire success of Italdesign, was partner Aldo Mantovani (1927–), a deeply experienced body engineer who had spent 19 years at Fiat with legendary engineer Dante Giacosa (1905–96) during the postwar boom years when Fiat was leading the way in production design. Thanks to Mantovani's involvement, Italdesign did not offer just exterior and interior designs, but a highly integrated engineering package that specified how the car was to be built, the design of the tooling, and a complete schedule for production.

The new Golf (initially sold as the Rabbit in the United States) was the complete antithesis of the Beetle. Gone were the baroque aerodynamics and curves, replaced by a crisp, fresh, geometric form around a 'post-Issigonis' 'super-mini' architecture. In one bound VW was free from the albatross of the ageing 'people's car' tag. The Golf was a hit from the outset, becoming VW's most important single product and the lynchpin of its rise to become Europe's number-one carmaker. Though modernized and reinvented several times since then, VW understands that the Golf's continuing evolution is a balancing act between the familiar and the novel, and each version still pays homage to Giugiaro's design invention.

Right: Crisp and almost perfect for the purpose. Giorgetto Giugiaro's original Golf let Volkswagen throw off the shackles of the quirky Beetle.

BMW 3 SERIES 1975

The progress of BMW has been, so far, an almost exemplary tale of brand development. The key to its present identity can quite clearly be found in the work of Giovanni Michelotti (1921–80), one of the most important, though lesser-known, figures in the Turin car design world.

By the early 1960s BMW production was split between expensive cars, nicknamed 'Baroque Angels' (*Barockengel*) on account of their florid, retro looks, and diminutive economy 'bubble' cars, which were based on the Italian Isetta design that BMW had licensed. BMW then tried mid-sized projects, which came of age with the handsome 1962 Neue Klasse 1500 series for which Michelotti provided the characteristic geometrical architecture and 'kidney grille' front end. These have remained the hallmarks of the brand ever since. Indeed, each new iteration of the 3 and 5 Series cars can be seen as a step in a progressive though quite gentle morphing (usually by lowering and rounding) of the essential Michelotti form.

Intriguingly, Michelotti deployed very similar language in his work for Triumph with the 1300 and Dolomite. But though these cars were attractive and widely admired, Triumph seemed not to have the quality and industrial consistency to equal BMW and it became part of the catastrophic decline of British Leyland and the UK car industry.

Right and below: BMW epitomizes a particular pattern of 'vertical' brand development in which every model respects a clear family architecture. The 3 Series is the German company's most important product line.

92

LANCIA MEGAGAMMA

'He really is a star – for the one-designer car, probably the best in the world right now.' History has not reversed this judgment on Giorgetto Giugiaro (1938–) , from Ghia studio boss Filippo Sapino, for Giugiaro proved that he was able to move from the world of high-concept show cars and feline supersports forms to designing and redefining the architecture of popular cars.

We are used now to 'people carriers', or MPVs, but when Giugiaro introduced the Megagamma in 1978 at the Turin Motor Show it was genuinely a new vehicle type. With this vehicle Giugiaro was the first to experiment with reversing the trend towards lowness and sportiness, realizing that increased height allows a different seat angle and improved roominess in small vehicles (a theme he later exploited with the Fiat Uno). Lancia/Fiat were not confident enough about sales to produce it, but homages to Giugiaro's concept such as the Nissan Prairie and Renault Espace were soon followed by similar offerings from most other makers, establishing this as one of the most popular vehicle types for family use today.

Right and below: Giorgetto Giugiaro pioneered the move back to higher cars with the 1978 Megagamma and paved the way for MPVs and 'people carriers'.

MAZDA RX7

The invention of the Wankel rotary triggered a gold rush among the world's automakers to acquire licences (see pages 80–81). Was the new Wankel rotary engine destined to be the future for personal transportation – or, as Chrysler's engineering boss Alan Loofbourrow predicted, would it turn out to be 'one of the most unbelievable fantasies ever to hit the world auto industry'?

General Motors saw it as the way ahead and thought so much of its new industrial secret that it cautioned, 'careless disclosure is detrimental, not only to the corporation, but to ... the employees themselves in a direct and personal way'. However, climbing oil prices and concern about emissions soon caused GM to drop the project, while NSU's pioneering Wankel Ro 80 car ran into deep trouble in Germany with serial engine failure caused by the compression seals of its units.

However, Toyo Kogyo (today Mazda) in Japan, alone among carmakers, kept to the belief that the Wankel could make a viable rotary engine through painstaking development. Even so, its researchers were sorely tried. 'Our top management courageously adopted a courageous mentality' was the very Japanese comment from chief engineer Kenichi Yamamoto on the years of trouble during which 'it was necessary to try out every possible material available on this earth'.

The culmination of this perseverance was the RX7 – reliable, fast and uncannily smooth, but also a curious comment on the nature of technological successions. Yet the Wankel cannot be written off, for social needs change and so do fuels. Mazda claim that its motor can burn hydrogen more efficiently and safely than regular piston engines, while not requiring the rare catalysts needed to use hydrogen in a fuel cell.

Right: Like a Galapagos turtle, the Mazda rotary-engined car has been pursuing its own lonely and particular development. Only time will show if it is an evolutionary dead end.

AUDI 100 1983

The creation of Audi as a premium German car brand is one of the great industrial achievements of the post-World War II era. In 1965 Auto Union, now based in Ingolstadt, Bavaria, revived the prewar Audi name, though shortly afterwards the group was bought by Volkswagen. In 1969 this group merged with NSU (forming Audi NSU Auto Union AG), and Audi was moved steadily upmarket, becoming the premium brand for the group and a name that would come to rival BMW and Mercedes. Through the 1970s and 1980s Audi would be steered largely by Ferdinand Piëch (1937–), whose judgment and instincts proved almost flawless. Piëch, of course, is a grandson of Ferdinand Porsche and grew up steeped in 'car culture'.

Design has been integral to the success of Audi and was directed at Ingolstadt by Hartmut Warkuss – an exceptional design director and manager who knew how to make the best use of many talented younger designers (including ex-Royal College of Art graduates Martin Smith and Peter Schreyer). The design department was also integrated very cleverly with the engineering department and together they worked to ensure that every model had a new technical edge, for Audi explicitly noted that Germany's high labour and social costs made the cars expensive, 'so we have to justify the price with excellent technology'. One such feature was full-time four-wheel drive in a saloon car (a first for series production). Another was the body development that made the renewed Audi 100 one of the most aerodynamically efficient full saloon cars on the market, with a drag coefficient of 0.30 – still a good figure today.

Right and below: The rebirth of Audi in the teeth of competition from existing high-end German brands was a brilliant achievement. Audi sought always to give each model a particular technical edge.

TOYOTA PRIUS

The Prius shows an extraordinary commitment to a new technology from a major manufacturer, Toyota. There seems little doubt that it was the personal conviction of Dr Shoichiro Toyoda, president of the company, that drove this, for he is on record as stating, some time before such views became commonplace, that CO_2 emissions and global warming were the greatest problems facing mankind.

The hybrid-drive Prius uses a petrol (gasoline) engine plus two electric motors/generators and a substantial battery pack to allow it to run with electrical or engine power, or any proportion of both. Efficiency advantages come from the fact that the petrol engine only drives the road wheels via the electrical system and therefore always runs at its most efficient speed and power setting. Thus it never needs to run inefficiently at low speed or small throttle openings. Moreover, under deceleration the motors then function as dynamos, recovering kinetic energy and producing electrical power to charge the batteries. The efficiency of this set-up is a matter of ongoing debate.

The Prius performs well for fuel economy, but some users and reviewers suggest that a simple and efficient diesel engine will beat the more complex Prius on both consumption and on emissions, particularly when whole-life 'cradle to grave' build and disposal costs are compared. However, hybrid technology is new and constantly improving.

There is no doubt that the Prius is a technological tour de force, though its great success in locations such as London and California has been helped by favourable tax or charging regimes.

Right and below: The hybrid petrol–electric power plant is one route to an efficient car with low emissions. Toyota has made a brave and committed move to this new architecture.

FIAT MULTIPLA

The original Multipla was a joyous device conceived in 1956 by the incomparable Dante Giacosa (1905–96) to make an estate car out of his new Fiat 600. The rear-engine layout made this quite a trick, but Giacosa came up with a completely new vehicle type with three rows of seats, perfect for many families of modest means, and thereby anticipated the new typology of 'people carriers' by more than 20 years.

The new Multipla completely reversed this idea. By the 1990s long three-row 'van'-type people carriers were commonplace, so the challenge from Paolo Cantarella – at the time managing director of Fiat Auto – was to accommodate six people in comfort in a new short car under 4m (13ft) long.

Designer Roberto Giolito and his team came up with a unique variant – a wide vehicle accommodating three seats in the front and three behind. The two-row layout gave a far more congenial interior for some user groups, as well as a driving experience that was far superior to that of its van-like rivals.

Unfortunately, the intriguing 'frog face' front end repelled many people and earned it the 'Ugliest Car' award from the BBC's *Top Gear* in 1999, though the same programme also voted it 'Car of the Year' in 2000. Perhaps the lesson of this episode is that public expectations can be led gently to accept surprising new shapes, as Patrick Le Quément has shown at Renault. Fiat may have surprised the market too much with this daring new shape, but the Multipla is nonetheless destined to be a future automobile classic.

Right and below: The frog-faced Multipla with 3+3 seating was a clever design invention. Too bad that Fiat did not signal the arrival of the new shape with hints in earlier cars.

NISSAN CUBE 1998

Nissan is unusual in that it does not attempt a coherent and unifying visual identity across its range, proving that it is possible to break the rules of 'brand management' as exemplified by BMW and Mercedes. Each Nissan model appears to be a unique attempt to address a specific sector and conforms to its own aesthetic rules.

Although Nissan (formerly Datsun) spearheaded the Japanese invasion of Western markets, it later ran into problems until it was able to form a surprising association with Renault, acquiring Carlos Ghosn as President. Ghosn quickly headhunted Shiro Nakamura (1950–) from Isuzu as design director, a man who came with his own explicit agenda to base new designs on Japanese culture. Nakamura believes that 'Japan has centuries of tradition in the ability to combine an object's function and beauty in the best possible way, and the most interesting aspect is that this is reflected in extremely simple lines.'

The Cube, developed following these precepts by design leader Satoru Tai, is intended to reference a Japanese aesthetic through its use of straight lines and right angles, but it also signals a new maturity in urban car design and use. If speeds are slow, aerodynamics and sporty looks become irrelevant. Habitability and the congeniality of the internal space become more important and cars can become 'unashamedly cubic'. The extra height also contributes significantly to roominess, as Giorgetto Giugiaro (1938–) had demonstrated with his Megagamma back in 1978.

Right and below: The end of the sports car? The Cube reinvents design aesthetics, looking at city life today and arguing that, if speeds are low, roominess is much more important than aerodynamics.

SMART

During the 1980s Nicolas Hayek (1928–), as chief executive of the conglomerate Swatch Group, reformed the sprawling Swiss watch industry, restoring profit and a sense of desirability to both premium brands and its popular Swatch range. The spearhead of the campaign was the creation of the Swatch watch itself as an affordable, ever-changing fashion brand, made by highly integrated computer design and manufacturing techniques.

Hayek also envisioned a low-cost micro car as a new Swatch product. This would be built in a fresh way to preserve the virtuous Swatch high-speed link from a fermenting graphic and general design department to the production line, spawning an infinitely refreshed range of visually cheeky personal cars, powered, moreover, by an eco-friendly electric or hybrid power source.

An early association with Volkswagen did not work out so in 1994 Swatch and Mercedes-Benz teamed up to build the car. The low cost for the product expected by Hayek proved hubristic, for the mainstream auto industry has had decades of experience of driving down the cost of a complex product to an absurdly low level. There were really no new ways to reduce the cost below that of a conventional Panda- or Polo-sized car. Since the introduction of the Smart, Mercedes-Benz is considered to have lost some $4 billion in the venture. However, it still hopes the range will become profitable and it has achieved something useful by inserting a new micro car type into the traffic ecology of cities. In some ways Smart has paid the penalty of going first – both Fiat's new 500 and Toyota's IQ show that those companies also believe there is now potential in this new sub-Mini sector.

Right: The arrival of the Smart is welcome, in the face of the almost irresistible growth in the bulk and weight of personal vehicles. However, it is unlikely that Mercedes-Benz will recover the huge investment that it has taken to install the Smart in our consciousness.

Figures in italics
indicate captions.

Adler 20
Alfa Romeo 30, *30*, 36, 46,
    48, *48*, 86
Alfa Romeo Portello works 48
Alfa Romeo-based Conguro
    82
Alfasud 86, *86*, 90
Aluminium Français 52
Amilcar 16
Anderloni, Felice Bianchi 30
argon-arc aluminium welding
    70
Aston Martin 30, 70, 74
Audi 80, *96*, 98, *98*
Austin 64, 86
    1100 64
    Allegro 86, *86*
    FX4 taxi 58, *58*
    Seven 12, *12*
    TX4 58
Austin, Herbert 12, *12*
Auto Union, Ingolstadt,
    Bavaria 98

Bache, David 84
Bailey, Eric 58
Barthes, Roland 54
BBC *Top Gear* 102
Benn, Tony 86
Bentley 70
Bertone 30, 48, 72, 78
    BAT 46, *46*
    Carabo show car 82, *82*
    Stratos 82
Bertone, Flaminio 54, *54*
Bertone, Giuseppe 'Nuccio'
    46, 48
Bizzarrini, Giotto 72
BMW 28, *30*, 92, 98, 104
    3 Series 92, *92*
    5 Series 92
    'Baroque Angels'
    (*Barockengel*) 92
    BMW 328 28, *28*
    Neue Klasse 1550 series 92

Boano, Mario 48
Boulanger, Pierre-Jules
    42, 54
Bristol 28, *28*, 30
British Aeroplane Company
    70
British leyland 92
British Motor Corporation
    (BMC) 64, 86
Broadley, Eric 74
Brooklands *10*, 16
Buckminster Fuller, Richard
    20, *20*
Buckower Dreieck *14*
Bugatti 14, *14*, 24, *24*
Bugatti, Carlo 14
Bugatti, Ettore 14, 24
Bugatti, Jean 24, *24*
Buick
    LeSabre concept car 44, *44*
Burzi, Dick 58

Cantarella, Paolo 102
Carrozzeria Touring 30
Castel Furano 50
Chapman, Colin 60, 74
chassis, rigid box section 28
Chevrolet
    Corvair 76, *76*
    Corvette Sting Ray 72
'chevron' gears 22
Chicago World Exposition
    (1933) 20
Chiswick, west London *16*
Chrysler 50, 96
Cisitalia 30, 32, 78, *78*, 86
    Berlinetta 32, *32*
Citroën 52, 80
    2CV 42, *42*, 68
    Ami 68, *68*
    DS 54, *54*, 68
    Traction Avant 18, 22, *22*
Citroën, André 22, 42
CO_2 emissions 100, *100*
Coles, Edward 76
Colombo, Gioachino 36
computer-modelling
    techniques 44

concept cars 44
Continental Alpine Trials 28
Corvair Testudo 82
Corvette 56
Costin, Frank 60
Coventry Climax engine 60, *60*
cyclecar 10, 12

Daimler-Benz 86, *106*
D'Ascanio, Corradino 40
Datsun 104
Davenport, Basil 10, *10*
de Havilland 60
Delage 24
Delahaye 24
Design Museum 6
Diesel, Rudolf 80
diesel engine 100
disc brakes 60
DKW 62, 66
dog clutches 10
Duncan, Isadora 16
Duroplast 62
Dusio, Piero 32
Dymaxion 20, *20*

Earl, Harley 44, *44*
Edward G. Budd Company
    of Philadelphia 22
eight-cylinder engine 14, 26,
    36, 74
electrical equipment 34
Enlightenment 8
ERA six-cylinder machine 36

Farina, Battista 'Pinin' 32
Fenaille, Pierre 18
Ferguson, Adam 8
Ferrari 32, 36, 60, 70, 72, 74,
    74, 78
Ferrari, Enzo 36, 74
Ferrari Maranello factory *36*
Fiat 32, 90
    500 *106*
    600 56, *56*, 102
    Auto 102
    Multipla 102, *102*
    Nuova 500

Panda 106
Turbina 50, *50*
Uno 94
flat-4 'boxer' engine 86
Ford 66
  Cortina 86
  GT 74
  GT 40 74, *74*
  Model T 8, *8*
Ford, Henry 8, 22
Ford, Henry, II 74, *74*
Fordism 8
Formula One design 12, 60
four-cylinder engine 12, 68
four-stroke motor 66
four-wheel brakes 26
four-wheel drive 84, 98
Frazer Nash cars 10, 28
Frazer-Nash, Archibald 10, *10*
front engine 20
front-wheel drive 18, 20, 22,
  22, 64, *66*

Gandini, Marcello 46, 82, *82*
gas turbine 50
gearbox, integrated 64
General Motors (GM) 44, *44*,
  80, 96
Ghosn, Carlos 104
Giacosa, Dante 56, *56*, 90, 102
Giugiaro, Giorgetto 46, 78, 82,
  86, *86*, 90, *90*, 94, *94*, 104
global warming 78, 100
Godfrey, Ronald 10
Godfrey & Nash (GN) 10, 12
  'Spider' 10, *10*
Gold Cup Oulton Park,
  Cheshire *74*
Grand Prix of Reggio Emilia 14
Grégoire, Jean-Albert 18, 52
Gropius, Walter 20
GT40 programme 74
Gulf Oil *74*

Hassan, Walter 70
Hayek, Nicolas 106
headlamps 54
Heusser, H. *14*

Highland Park factory (Ford)
  8, *8*
hill-climb 'specials' 10, *10*
Hitler, Adolf 8, 34
Honda 72
Hruska, Rudolf 86
hybrid power 100, *100*, 106

Iacocca, Lee 74
Isotta Fraschini 30
Issigonis, Alec 64, *64*, 86
Italdesign, Moncalieri, Turin
  86
'Italian line' 30, 32

Jaguar *6*, 32, 70, *70*, 86
Jano, Vittorio 36
Jaray, Paul 26, 34, 66
Jaray Streamline Carriage
  Company, Zurich 26
Jensen 30

Kahn, Albert *8*
KdF-Wagen (Volkswagen) 26
'kidney grille' 92
King, Charles Spencer 84
Kirwan-Taylor, Peter 60

Lamborghini
  350 GTV 72, *72*
  Countach 82, *82*
  Miura 78, *78*, 82
  V12 engine 72
Lamborghini, Ferruccio 72
Lampredi, Aurelio 36
Lancia
  Aprilia 30
  Megagamma 94, *94*
Land Rover 38, *38*, 84
Le Corbusier 6
Le Mans 16, 18, 30, *30*, 32,
  70, 74, *74*
Le Quément, Patrick 102
Ledwinka, Hans 26
Lefèbvre, André 22, 42, 54
Levallois-Perret, Paris 16
Leyland truck and bus
  company 86

Lingotto rooftop track 50
Lola Cars 74
Lola GT 74
London 'black cab' 58, *58*
London Motor Show (1948) 70
Longbridge Austin plant 86
Loofbourrow, Alan 96
Lord, Leonard 64
Lotus 60, *60*, 74, 78
LTI 58
Lyons, William 70

Magès, Paul 54
Mann, Harris 86
Mantovani, Aldo 90
Maserati 36, 60
Maserati brothers 30
Mays, J 74
Mazda
  MX-5 16
  RX7 96, *96*
Mercedes-Benz 98, 104, 106
MG 16
Michelin tyre company 42
Michelotti, Giovanni 92
mid-engined cars 78, *78*
Mini 64, *64*
Miramas circuit, southern
  France *16*
Modernism 66
Molsheim factory, Alsace 14,
  24
monocoque
  glass-fibre 60
  integrated structural 78
Monte Carlo Rally 66, *66*
Monza 50
Morris 64, 86
Mors 22
Moss, Stirling 36
Moulon, Alex 64

Nader, Ralph: *Unsafe at
  Any Speed* 44
Nakamura, Shiro 104
Nash 58
Nervi, Pier Luigi 46
Nissan 104

Cube 104, *104*
Prairie 94
S Cargo 6
NSU 98
Ro 80 car 80, *80*, 96
Nuvolari, Tazio 86

off-road 'trials' 12
Offficine Meccanische (OM)
86
open tourers
Otto, Nikolaus 80

Panhard Dyna 52, *52*
Paris Motor Show (1948) 42
'people carriers' 102
Petit, Emile *16*
Piaggio Ape 40, *40*
Piëch 84
Piëch, Ferdinand 98
Pininfarina 30, 32
Pomigliano d'Arco, near
Naples 86
Porsche 26, 84
Porsche, Ferdinand 34, 86, 98
pressed-steel body 22, *22*
Prinetti & Stucchi 14
production line 8
propeller shaft 26
Public Carriage Office,
London 58, *58*

'Quartic' wheel 86

racing cars 12
Range Rover 84, *84*
Rapi, Luigi Fabio 50
rear engine 20, 26, 76, 90
rear-wheel drive 20
Renault 102, 104
Espace 94
'Retrofuturism' programme 74
Rolls-Royce 38, 84
Rome Grand Prix 50
Rover company 38, 50, 86

Saab 96 66, *66*
'safety bicycle' 38

Salmson 'San Sebastian' 16,
16
Salomano, Carlo 50
Sapino, Filippo 94
Sason, Sixten 66
Sayer, Malcolm 70
Scaglione, Franco 46, 48, 72,
72
Schreyer, Peter 98
Segre, Luis 48
semiautomatic epicyclic
transmission 8
Setright, L.J.K. 42
Shelby, Carroll 74
six-cylinder engine 28, *28*, 70
Skegness, Lincolnshire *10*
Smart 106, *106*
Smith, Martin 98
Société des Automobiles
Tracta 18
sports versions 12
Stalin, Joseph 8
Starley, John Kemp 38
Stokes, Donald 86
streamlining 24, 26
styling bridge 44
suspension
front 66
hydraulic suspension 54
independent 26, 60, 78
long-travel 84
Svensk Flygmotor 66
Swatch Group 106
swing axles 34

Tai, Satoru 104
Tatra 34
T87 26, *26*
Topolino 56
Touring coachwork
company, Milan 32, 72, *72*
Touring Superleggera
construction system 30
Toyo Kogyo (now Mazda) 96
Toyoda, Dr Shoichiro 100
Toyota
IQ 106
Prius 100, *100*

Trabant 62, *62*
Trabant Zwickau works 62
'Trabbie' (Trabant) *62*
Tracta 18, *18*, 52
transverse engine 64
Triumph 86
1300 92
Dolomite 92
trucks, light 40, *40*
Turin Motor Show 46, 48, 72, 94
twelve-cylinder engine 36
twin-cam engine 16, 48
two-cylinder engine 10
two-stroke motor 62, *62*

Übelacker, Erich 26

Vespa 40
Vintage Sports Car Club 10
Voisin, Gabriel 22
Volkswagen 26, *76*, 86, 96, 106
Beetle 34, *34*, 56, 76, 90
'Fastback' estate car
('Variant') 90
K70 saloon 90
Polo 106
VW Golf (Rabbit) 90, *90*
Volkswagen Wolfsburg plant
34

Wankel, Felix 80
Wankel rotary engine 80, *80*,
96
Warkuß, Hartmut 98
Weber carburettor barrels 78
Weslake, Harry 70
Whittle, Frank 38
Wilks, Maurice 38, 84
Wilks, Spencer 84
Willys Jeep 38
Wilson, Harold 86
Wyer, John 74, *74*

XK engine 70

Yamamoto, Kenichi 96

Zeppelin 26, 34

PICTURE CREDITS

The publisher would like to thank the following contributors for their kind permission to reproduce the following photographs:

2 Thierry Brisacque/ Gamma/ Eyedea/Camera Press London; 7 Jaguar Daimler Heritage Trust; 9 Top Hulton Archive/Getty Images; 9 Bottom Three Lions/Getty Images; 11 Top National Motor Museum/MPL; 11 Bottom FPG/Hulton Archive/ Getty Images; 12-13 General Photographic Agency/Getty Images; 14-15 akg-images; 16-17 Andrew Nahum Archive; 19 National Motor Museum/MPL; 20-21 Courtesy of The Estate of R. Buckminster Fuller; 23 Citroen Communication; 24-25 Car Culture/Getty Images; 26 National Motor Museum/ MPL; 27 Kees Smit; 28-29 BMW AG; 30 Courtesy of Giovanni Bianchi Anderloni; 31 Alfa Romeo; 33 Top National Motor Museum/ MPL; 33 Bottom Jerry Cooke/Time Life Pictures/ Getty Images; 34 Hulton Archive/Getty Images; 35 akg-images; 36-37 Ferrari SpA; 39 Tif Hunter; 40-41 Piaggio; 42 Transtock Inc/Alamy; 43 Keystone-France/Camera Press; 45 Used with permission of General Motors Media Archives/General Motors Corp.; 46-47 Bertone; 48-49 Alfa Romeo; 50 National Motor Museum/MPL; 51 Fiat; 52 Andrew Nahum Archive; 53 National Motor Museum/ MPL; 55 Citroen Communication; 56-57 Fiat; 59 Malcolm/Hulton Archive/ Getty Images; 61 Sutton Motorsport Images/Heritage-Images; 62 akg-images; 63 Popperfoto/Getty Images; 64 British Motor Industry Heritage Trust; 65 BMW AG; 67 SAAB; 68-69 Citroen Communication; 71 Jaguar Daimler Heritage Trust; 72 Car Culture/Getty Images; 73 Klemantaski Collection/Getty Images; 74-75 Ford Motor Company; 77 Used with permission of General Motors Media Archives/General Motors Corp.; 79 Tom Wood/Alamy; 80-81 Tif Hunter; 82 Andrew Nahum Archive; 83 Alfa Romeo; 85 British Motor Industry Heritage Trust; 86-87 Alfa Romeo; 89 Keystone/Hulton Archives/Getty Images; 91 Volkswagen; 92-93 BMW AG; 94-95 Italdesign Giugiaro SpA; 97 Mazda; 98-99 Audi; 100-101 National Motor Museum/MPL; 102-103 Fiat; 104-105 Simon Clay/ Alamy; 107 Lawrence Jackson/AP/PA Photos

Every effort has been made to trace the copyright holders and we apologise in advance for any unintentional errors or omissions, and would be pleased to insert the appropriate acknowledgment in any subsequent publication.

CREDITS

An Hachette UK Company
www.hachette.co.uk

First published in Great
Britain in 2009 by Conran
Octopus Ltd, a division
of Octopus Publishing
Group Ltd, in conjunction
with the Design Museum

This edition published in 2016

Octopus Publishing
Group Ltd
Carmelite House
50 Victoria Embankment
London EC4Y 0DZ
www.octopusbooks.co.uk
www.octopusbooksusa.com

Distributed in the US by
Hachette Book Group
1290 Avenue of the
Americas, 4th and 5th Floors,
New York, NY 10020

Distributed in Canada by
Canadian Manda Group
664 Annette St., Toronto,
Ontario, Canada M6S 2C8

A CIP catalogue record
for this book is available
from the British Library.

Publisher:
Lorraine Dickey
Consultant Editor:
Deyan Sudjic
Managing Editor:
Sybella Stephens
Editor:
Robert Anderson

Art Director:
Jonathan Christie
Design:
Untitled
Picture Researcher:
Anne-Marie Hoines

Production Controller:
Allison Gonsalves

Printed and bound in China

ISBN 978 1 84091 734 5

10 9 8 7 6 5 4 3 2 1

Text written by: Andrew Nahum

Andrew Nahum is Principal Curator of
Technology and Engineering at the Science
Museum, London and is a research tutor in
the Department of Vehicle Design at the Royal
College of Art. He has written extensively
on the history of technology, aviation and
transport for both scholarly and popular
journals.

The Design Museum is one of the world's
leading museums of contemporary design.
Design Museum Members enjoy free
unlimited entry to the museum's outstanding
exhibitions as well as access to events,
tours and discounts. Becoming a Member
is an inspiring way to support the museum's
work. Visit designmuseum.org/become-a-
member and get involved today.